Battlegrou

Frank

and the

Defence of Arras

1940

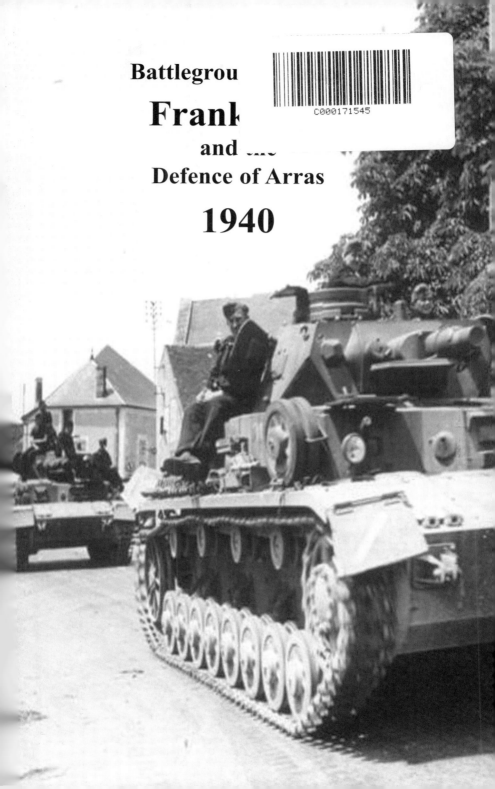

Battleground Series

Battleground Europe

Frankforce

and the
Defence of Arras

1940

Jerry Murland

Series Editor
Nigel Cave

Pen & Sword
MILITARY

First published in Great Britain in 2017 by
Pen & Sword Military
An imprint of
Pen & Sword Books Ltd
47 Church Street
Barnsley
South Yorkshire
S70 2AS

ISBN 978 147385 269 3

The right of Jerry Murland to be identified as Author
of this work has been asserted by him in accordance with the
Copyright, Designs and Patents Act 1988.

A CIP catalogue record for this book is
available from the British Library.

Typeset in Times New Roman by Chic Graphics

Printed and bound in England by
CPI Group (UK) Ltd., Croydon, CR0 4YY

Pen & Sword Books Ltd incorporates the imprints of
Pen & Sword Archaeology, Atlas, Aviation, Battleground, Discovery,
Family History, History, Maritime, Military, Naval, Politics,
Railways, Select, Social History, Transport, True Crime,
Claymore Press, Frontline Books, Leo Cooper, Praetorian Press,
Remember When, Seaforth Publishing and Wharncliffe.

For a complete list of Pen & Sword titles please contact
PEN & SWORD BOOKS LIMITED
47 Church Street, Barnsley, South Yorkshire, S70 2AS, England
E-mail: enquiries@pen-and-sword.co.uk
Website: www.pen-and-sword.co.uk

Contents

List of Maps

Introduction by Series Editor

Devoted to the short-lived Frankforce, this book is geographically in an area associated with the 1914-1919 BEF and in particular Third Army. Place names and features will be readily recognised with those whose interest lies primarily in the Great War; it will add considerable further interest to battlefield tours, albeit concerning fighting that lasted, at best, only a few days.

In my early days of systematic battlefield touring, now (alas) over thirty years ago, I was introduced to the events of the latter days of May 1940 in the Arras area by the finest battlefield guide I have known, Tony Spagnoly. Although the visit was primarily to the Great War battlefields around Arras, he touched upon one or two events during the fighting there less than twenty five years later.

One story he recounted was of a couple of men of the Durham Light Infantry who were having a quick drink in a café in Wancourt; they were shot as they emerged by a machine gun mounted on a motor bike side car. The proprietress of the bar, whose family owned the bar then, remembered the events of 20 May vividly. The soldiers now lie, with several unknown from the campaign, in the communal cemetery. Further afield, in the typically unassuming Artois hamlet of La Herlière, about twenty kilometres south west of Arras and off the Doullens road, lies Private Lungley of the 5th Buffs, killed on 20 May and buried in the communal cemetery. In death he is accompanied by two soldiers from the Great War.

John Lungley came from Worthing, which added to the interest for my father, who then lived there. His battalion was a unit in the rather unfortunate 12th (Eastern) Division, whose men were ill trained, ill equipped and had been rushed to France. It was part of 36 Brigade, which was severely mauled during the fighting. Gregory Blaxland, in his *Destination Dunkirk*, devoted some lines to John Lungley. He comments that, despite the miserable outcome of the fighting, the locals who remained to view the fighting received a badly needed boost to their morale to sustain them for the coming years:

Certainly at La Herlière a lone deed of defiance by a young British soldier lightened the sullen gloom of the subsequent occupation. His name was Private Lungley ... his Bren could be heard to chatter out his answer to shouted demands for his surrender. A tank had to be brought up to kill him and he was buried in the hole from which he had fought. The villagers emulated his defiance of German orders by nightly laying flowers on his grave, and they turned out with such fervour for his reburial in the village cemetery that the Germans, in great anger, stopped the ceremony. Instead, it took place secretly at night. The pride of the people had been rekindled, and this was an achievement of far greater value than anything measurable in terms of casualties inflicted or delays imposed.

I had done quite a bit of work on the dead of my old school in the Great War; however, this did not preclude reading some of the moving obituaries of those who lost their life in the Second War. Amongst these was John Radford of 2/Wilts, he was of particular interest to me because his father, also an old boy, was awarded the MC in the previous conflict whilst serving in the Royal Field Artillery; and who then became the commander of the school's OTC when it was re-established after the outbreak of hostilities. Supplied with his details by the CWGC, on one of my annual battlefield visits I made the diversion to Pelves (a place of some note in the 1917 Battle of Arras). He lies in the little communal cemetery, close to the River Scarpe, along with two others from his battalion.

A more recent contact with those caught up in the German onslaught of 1940 came in the late 1990s when I was examining an extension of the Grange Subway at Vimy, a section of it closed to the public. As part of a Durand Group investigation, I was seeing if a way could be dug through a blockage to what on the map was shown to be a series of rooms that served as a company – and on 9 April 1917 as a battalion – headquarters. The endeavour came to nought; but I was able to admire the graffiti that had been carved into the chalk by British troops whiling away the hours in that late spring of 1940. More poignant was that of refugees – a fair number of whom seem to have been Belgian – who also left their mark on the wall of a gallery that had been dug to fight another war. Alas, access to this area is now firmly blocked.

The cases of those men of the DLI, of John Lungley and John Radford underline a point made by Jerry in this fine book about the men of Frankforce: the little communal cemeteries in the area often hold one or two graves from the fighting of May 1940 and doubtless they are very rarely visited. Since so many come to this part of France on tours of the battlefields of the Great War, it would seem fitting to take the time to stop occasionally and visit these isolated burials of the sons of soldiers, many of whom who would have fought over these same fields and who could scarcely have imagined that the whole, ghastly process was to be repeated well within the lifetime of most of them.

Nigel Cave
Ratcliffe College

Author's Introduction

There is no other city in France that has the same associations in time of conflict that the British have with Arras. Since the campaigns of John Churchill, 1st Duke of Marlborough, in the early 18th century, British soldiers have fought in and around Arras, occasionally as an enemy but, more often, as defenders of French and Allied democracy. Battlefield visitors to the area will immediately recognize the names of towns and villages that were as significant to the men of Marlborough's army as they were to those who fought in the First and Second World Wars.

Arras lies in a hollow on a large chalk plain in northern France, with Vimy Ridge to the north and the River Scarpe valley to the west and east. Established by the Gaul tribes during the Iron Age, the first mention of the name *Arras* appeared in the 12th century, possibly originating from the Celtic word *Ar,* meaning running water. Today it is the third largest conurbation in the Pas-de-Calais after Calais and Boulogne-sur-Mer, with

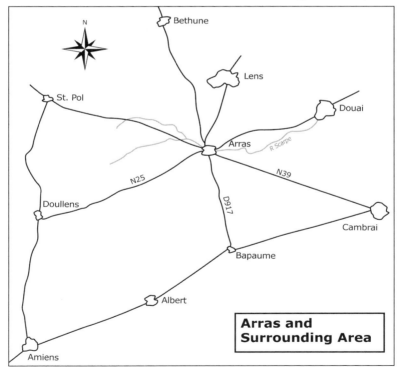

a population of nearly 44,000. Well known for its architecture, culture and history, the city is twinned with Ipswich in Suffolk and Oudenaarde in Belgium.

Early history

Originally named by the Romans *Nemetacum,* (and later *Atrebatum*), Arras rose to prominence as an important garrison town renowned for its arts and crafts. In the late 4th century the inhabitants were converted to Christianity and an episcopal see and monastic community were established by Saint Vaast. In 667 the building of Abbey Saint Vaast became the catalyst for the modern city of Arras to develop and, despite the later attacks by the Vikings in the 9th century, the city became an important cultural and commercial centre and was granted a commercial charter by the French crown in 1180.

The city hosted the Congress of Arras in 1435 in an unsuccessful attempt to end the Hundred Years' War. After the death of Duke **Charles the Bold** of Burgundy in 1477, King **Louis XI** of France besieged Arras. In an effort to erase the city's identity completely, Louis renamed it temporarily *Franchise* but ten years later the city was bequeathed to the Spanish Habsburgs as part of the Spanish Netherlands. Arras remained under Habsburg rule from 1493 until 1640, when it was captured again by the French. The Spanish ceded it by the peace treaty in 1659 and it has since remained French.

In 1780 **Maximilien de Robespierre**, a French lawyer and politician born in Arras and, one of the best-known and most influential figures of the revolutionary period, was elected fifth deputy of the Third Estate of Artois to the Estates-General in 1789. From September 1793 to July 1794, during the Reign of Terror, the city was under the supervision of **Joseph Lebon,** who implemented food restrictions, ordered 400 executions and destroyed several religious monuments, including Arras Cathedral and the Abbey of Saint Vaast.

Marlborough and the Ne Plus Ultra Lines

The war of 1701 between Britain and France stemmed largely from Louis XIV's political ambitions, but by 1708 the Duke of Marlborough, and Prince Eugene of Savoy had defeated the French at Blenhein, Ramillies and Oudenaarde and pushed France towards collapse. However, a renewed defiance by **Louis XIV** led to a second British campaign in Flanders led by the Duke in 1711. The most tangible demonstration of this defiance was the Ne Plus Ultra Lines, a system of fortifications, entrenchments and inundations, which blocked the way to Paris and stretched from Cambrai to the coast. Constructed under the direction of

Claude de Villars, the line drew its name from the need to prevent the further advance of Marlborough's army and at Arras ran along the River Scarpe. Here Marlborough demonstrated his strategic and tactical brilliance by unbalancing Villars with a march from the eastern end of the lines to Vimy, and then dashing eastwards again to penetrate the lines at Arleux. Misleading Villers over the importance he attached to Arleux, Marlborough allowed the small town and its causeway to fall into French hands, while he embarked on yet another deceptive manoeuvre. Splitting his army into three, he stealthily led his main force back to regain the causeways at Arleux and Aubencheul-au-Bac. Guarding his rear with a strong force

John Churchill, 1ˢᵗ Duke of Marlborough.

and refusing to do battle with Villars, Marlborough then laid siege to Bouchain, (which surrendered on 12 September), thus consolidated his opening through the NePlus Ultra Lines.

The First World War

Apart from the German cavalry incursion into Arras on 6 September 1914, the city remained west of the front line for the rest of the war and, although badly damaged by German shellfire, retained its integrity as an allied bastion. From October 1914 German forces held the high ground in Artois, which included Vimy Ridge and the plateau of Notre Dame de Lorette, from where they dominated French forces from Lens to Arras. In an effort to take the Lorette plateau the French launched the **First Battle of Artois** in 1914 which, although it failed to alter the status quo, did not prevent the French from embarking on the **Second Battle of Artois**, which began on 9 May 1915. On this occasion the French managed to reach the crest of Vimy Ridge before they were finally forced to retreat; but they did take the Lorette plateau from the Germans after days of brutal close quarter fighting. On 25 September 1915, the **Third Battle of Artois** commenced in conjunction with a large–scale British attack at Loos further north. A huge bombardment of five days preceded the infantry advance towards the village of Souchez but ultimately failed to secure Vimy Ridge.

In 1916, British and Commonwealth troops took over this part of the line from the French. The **Battle of Arras** (9 April to 16 May 1917) was a largely British offensive on a broad front running from Vimy Ridge in

British troops in the Grand Place in 1917.

the north to Bullecourt in the south. There were big gains on the first day, particularly on Vimy Ridge, which was successfully taken by the Canadian Corps and the British 24th Division. The Third Army in the centre advanced astride the Scarpe River, making the deepest penetration into German held territory since 1914, while in the south the Fifth Army attacked the Hindenburg Line, where they made only minimal gains. The British then engaged in a series of small-scale operations to consolidate the new positions and although these battles were generally successful, they failed to achieve the hoped for breakthrough.

On 28 March 1918, twenty-nine German divisions attacked the British Third Army on a ten mile front between Authuille and Oppy, with Arras and Vimy Ridge as the principal objectives. **Operation *Mars*** was one of a number of German offensives fought in the Spring of 1918, with the intention of ending the war before the arrival of the Americans. Fortunately, the British at Arras were far more prepared than the unfortunate Fifth Army further south, and the attack stalled within days against a well dug in defensive force. Arras remained firmly in Allied hands until the Armistice in November 1918.

The Second World War

After war was declared on 3 September 1939, the British Expeditionary Force (BEF) were back at Arras, where they established General Head Quarters (GHQ) in Palais-St-Vaast. During the short British occupation and defence, the city was badly damaged by German bombing and the last British troops evacuated the city on 23/24 May. After the D-Day landings in June 1944, the British Guards Armoured Division formally re-entered Arras on 1 September.

Material concerning the deployment of the units at Arras in 1940 has come from a variety of sources, including regimental histories and unit war diaries. While the war diaries give an overall picture of daily events, the reader should be aware that frequently these diaries were completed after the event and are not always entirely accurate. It is also regrettable that all too often regimental historians relied on the information contained in these diaries. Personal diary accounts are usually a little more accurate in content but are sometimes difficult to match with events that took place

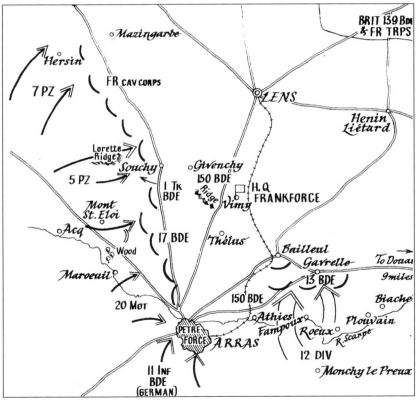

The threat to Arras showing the advance of German units from the west and south.

on a wider strategic front. However, Major Alan Coleman's diary is not only accurate but provides a humorous element into what must have been a harrowing time for the Arras garrison. Similarly, the accounts by Second Lieutenants Tony Younger and Rhidian Llewellyn provide us with two accurate accounts of events that took place south of the main railway line in Arras. The deployments of battalions along the Scarpe has again drawn on unit war diaries and regimental histories, but has also benefitted from personal accounts found amongst the 1970 Royal Tank Corps Battlefield Tour papers at the Imperial War Museum. These personal reminiscences have also brought the attack of 21 May to life by providing details from officers of both sides of the conflict that hitherto have been left out of published accounts of the fighting around Arras.

In Appendix 1 the reader will find notes on the various tanks referred to in the text and, in particular, the thickness of armour plating, which was a vital factor in armoured conflict. Appendix 2 provides a list of cemeteries in the wider Arras area that are outside the scope of this book, but where casualties from the May 1940 conflict can be visited. Appendix 3 is an abbreviated version of the Order of Battle for Arras in May 1940, although further details of each unit involved can be found in the relevant chapter. The ranks given to each individual are those that were held in May 1940 and do not reflect any subsequent promotion.

When describing the fighting I have often referred to modern day road numbering in order to give the reader using current maps of the area a more precise location. While some of the abbreviations in the text are self explanatory, others do require a modicum of explanation. I have used a form of abbreviation when describing units and formations; for example, after its first mention in the text 1st Battalion Welsh Guards becomes the 1/Welsh Guards or more simply the Welsh Guards and the 8th Royal Northumberland Fusiliers becomes 8/RNF. German army units are a little more complex. Within the infantry regiment there were three battalions – each one approximately the size of a British battalion – and, as with their British counterparts, the battalion was broken down into four companies of riflemen, who were given an Arabic numeral, for example, 3 *Kompanie*. Again, I have abbreviated when describing these units, thus the 7th Rifle Regiment becomes IR7, while the second battalion within that regiment is abbreviated to II/IR7; or, in the case of panzer regiments, II/Pz5. In the same way, the 78th Artillery Regiment is abbreviated to AR 78.

The Royal Tank Regiment began life as the Heavy Section Machine Gun Corps, which had gone into battle with the first tanks on the Somme in September 1916. Twenty-four years later the regiment had adopted the mantle of armoured warfare professionals and wore the badge of a First World War tank on their black berets. In 1939 The Royal Tank Corps joined with the newly mechanised cavalry to form the Royal Armoured Corps and the Corps' name was changed to Royal Tank Regiment to reflect cavalry terminology. It should be noted that it was not until September 1945 that the designation 'battalion' was officially removed from the title. After that date, the 4th and 7th Battalions of the Royal Tank Regiment became 4th and 7th Royal Tank Regiment. However, the shortened version was in use well before that time, and for simplicity, I have referred to them as 4/RTR and 7/RTR.

Equivalent German and British ranks referred to in the text are as follows:

Lieutenant General	*Generaloberst, General der Panzertruppe, Obergruppenführer*
Major General	*Generalmajor*
Colonel	*Oberst*
Lieutenant Colonel	*Oberstleutnant*
Major	*Major, Sturmbannführer*
Captain	*Hauptmann, Hauptsturmführer*
Lieutenant	*Oberleutnant*
Second Lieutenant	*Leutnant*
Corporal	*Unteroffizier*
Lance Corporal	*Gefreiter*
Infantry Private	*Infanterist, Schütze*

Acknowledgements

Arras has always been a special place for me. Two members of my family were decorated for gallantry during the 1917 offensive, and it was to Arras that I made my first battlefield visit. Since then I have visited the Arras battlefields on countless occasions and have frequently been accompanied by likeminded individuals such as, Jon Cooksey, Dave Rowland, Paul Webster, Bill Dodds, Peter Huxford and the late Rob Howard. To them I extend my thanks and gratitude for their company and enthusiasm and for sharing those moments at the end of the day when the first beer is poured. However, it is only more recently that I have visited Arras with the intention of exploring the 1940 battlegrounds and, while this has opened up a whole new dimension of discovery, it has underlined the fact that the ground fought over during the First World War was, once again, the scene of fighting twenty-two years later. One only has to visit the CWGC Cemeteries that are liberally dotted around Arras to see the dead from both wars buried together in the same plot.

A book of this nature can only be written with the help and assistance of others and I must thank André Coilliot for his help in tracing the path of 70 Brigade and the Sauterne family for conducting me around Pronier Farm. Jon Cooksey has been equally helpful in not only lending me the 1982 Royal Tank Regiment Battlefield Tour material, but by maintaining his composure as I constantly redirected him to 1940 battlefield sites when we were supposed to be researching another topic altogether! I am most grateful to Trefor Llewellyn, who very kindly sent me the account of his father's stay in Arras with the Welsh Guards; to Jim Tuckwell, who has assisted me with the nominal rolls for the Durham Light Infantry; and the WW2 Talk Forum, who have answered my queries and assisted me in numerous other ways. In particular, Andrew Newson has been extremely helpful in sending me copies of the more obscure war diaries from his collection.

Finally my thanks must also go to the Imperial War Museum, the National Archives at Kew, the National Army Museum, the Durham County Record Office and my wife Joan, who has tolerated my absence across the water with her usual understanding and tolerance. Photographs have largely come from my own personal collection but a number have been taken by my eldest granddaughter, Alisha, who accompanied me to Arras during the summer of 2016.

Jerry Murland
Coventry 2016

Chapter One

Invasion

On 10 May 1940 Germany invaded France and the low countries of Holland, Belgium and Luxembourg. The attack involved three Army Groups advancing simultaneously; Army Group B, under *Generaloberst* Fedor von Bock, advanced through north eastern Belgium and a panzer assault, led by *Generaloberst* Gerd von Runstedt's Army Group A, which attacked through the Ardennes to cross the Meuse with the intention of cutting through the British and French armies. The third group, Army Group C under *Generaloberst* Wilhelm Ritter von Leeb, was tasked with breaking through the Maginot Line. Dubbed 'the Matador's Cloak' by Basil Liddell Hart, the German plan was masterly in its simplicity and adopted the code word *Fall Gelb*.

Generaloberst **Gerd von Rundstedt, commanded Army Group A.**

Up until 10 May Allied forces, under the overall command of General Maurice Gamelin, had concentrated on extending

The eight month period of the Phoney War lulled the Allies into a false sense of security.

the Maginot Line along the Belgian border, a period of some eight months that became known as the 'Phoney War'. Gamelin's plan to counter the expected German invasion was for French and British forces to cross the border into Belgium and occupy the line of the River Dyle, which runs roughly north and south about thirty miles east of Brussels. Given the operational code name Plan D, the British Expeditionary Force (BEF) were to deploy between Louvain and Wavre, with the French First Army, under General Georges Blanchard, on their right in the Gembloux Gap. The Belgians, who were expected to hold their positions for several days, would then fall back into the gap between the left of the BEF and the right of the General Henri Giraud's Seventh Army, who were to link-up with the Dutch via Breda.

General Maurice Gamelin was in overall command of Allied forces until he was replaced by Maxime Wegand on 17 May.

It was a plan that certainly puzzled many in the BEF who had spent the whole of the previous winter preparing defences behind the Belgian frontier. Now, as soon as Germany invaded Belgium, all that was to be abandoned and the enemy was to be brought to battle from positions that were unfamiliar and where the defences were already thought to be of a

General Henri Giraud.

General Georges Blanchard.

poor quality. If that was not bad enough, there was considerable doubt over the fighting quality of the Belgian forces and their ability to put up a stout resistance.

The BEF command structure

In overall command of the BEF was 53-year-old John Vereker, the 6th Viscount Gort. Known more simply as Lord Gort, he was a highly decorated Grenadier Guards officer who had served in the First World War with some distinction; wounded on four occasions, he had been decorated with the Military Cross (MC) and the Distinguished Service Order (DSO) and two bars. His award of the coveted Victoria Cross (VC) came whilst he was commanding the 1st Battalion during the battle on the Canal du Nord in 1918.

Commanding I Corps was General Sir John Dill, an individual who had served with distinction under Douglas Haig and succeeded General

John Vereker, 6ᵗʰ Viscount Gort and his Chief of Staff, Lieutenant General Henry Pownall, at Habarcq Château in November 1939.

Sir Edmund Ironside as Chief of the Imperial General Staff (CIGS) on 27 May 1940. After Dill's recall, command of I Corps was passed to Lieutenant General Michael Barker. In command of II Corps was the energetic and able Lieutenant General Alan Brooke, a gunner who rose from lieutenant to lieutenant colonel over the four years of the First World War. By the end of 1939 a third regular division had been formed – the 5th Division – and in January 1940 the first of the Territorial divisions arrived, giving rise to the formation of III Corps under the command of Lieutenant General Sir Ronald Adam.

The Dyle Line
The German advance of 10 May signalled the end of the 'Phoney War' and the move east by allied forces to the River Dyle. The main fighting force was headed by motorcycle units of the 4/Royal Northumberland

Fusiliers and the Morris CS9 Armoured Cars of the 12th Lancers and was carried out with little interference from enemy activity by the troop carrying companies of the Royal Army Service Corps (RASC). Gort's plan was to place the 1st and 2nd Divisions on the right flank and the 3rd Division on the left, astride Louvain. By way of reserve the 48th (South Midland) Division was ordered to move east of Brussels and the 4th and 50th (Northumbrian) Divisions to the south. In addition the 44th (Home Counties) Division was under orders to march to the Escaut south of Oudenaarde and the 42nd (East Lancashire) Division placed on readiness to take up station to their right if required.

General Headquarters

GHQ, as it was known, was situated at the château at Habarcq and at Arras, where it was based in the Palais-St-Vaast. The Hon Arthur Maxwell Stamp was a staff officer at Arras and remembered it was composed of 'a weird assortment of officers and men, with all sorts of jobs and specialities, the city was seething with khaki'. On 10 May Gort advanced with the BEF into Belgium and GHQ was moved to Wahagnies, where the forward command post was established. Remaining in Arras was GHQ (Rear) under the command of the Adjutant General, Lieutenant General Sir Douglas Brownrigg.

Lieutenant General Sir Douglas Brownrigg.

Events on the Meuse

The campaign was essentially lost on 14 May when German panzer units of Army Group A stormed across the Meuse and headed for the channel ports along a twenty-five mile wide corridor of advance. This was the so-called 'Sickle Cut' through the Ardennes, which reached the Channel coast on 20 May and effectively cut the Allied armies in two. These German advances late on 13 May had hastened a disorganized French retreat, which twenty-four hours later had been reduced to a rout, opening up a dangerous gap that ultimately the French failed to fill. General Georges Blanchard had little choice but to order a retirement to avoid being outflanked, which, in its turn, involved the British I Corps swinging their line back from the Dyle for some six miles to the River Lasane in order to conform to the French retirement. Gamelin was replaced by the

4

73-year-old General Maxime Weygand on 19 May; but by then, the military disaster of 1940 was almost complete.

Petreforce

On 17 May, Gort issued his orders for the defence of Arras and twenty-four hours later created the first of two 'ad hoc' formations that would have a direct impact on the fighting in and around Arras. Petreforce, under the command of 53-year-old Major General Roderick Petre, was created to hold Arras; unlike Macforce and its commander, Major General Mason McFarlane, Petre was already in command of the 12th Division and possessed a relatively experienced staff and system of communications. Unfortunately, his departure was not communicated to the 12th Division, who were by this time spread widely across the battlefield, and command appeared to rest with Petre's senior staff officer. Failing to inform the 12th Division that Petre was now commanding 'Petreforce' and thus leaving it for the most part leaderless, was just one example of a patchwork of ineptitude on the part of the 54-year-old Adjutant General, Sir Douglas Brownrigg, that was to seal the fate of the 12th Division's battalions and the majority of 70 Brigade from the 23rd Division.

73-year-old General Maxime Weygand was recalled from North Africa to take over command of the Allied Armies.

General André Corap.

A deteriorating situation

By19 May the strategic situation in the French First Army Group had become serious. To the north Allied forces had been forced back to the line of the River Escaut, while in the south the Panzer advance of Army Group A, that had broken through at Sedan, had created a large gap in General André Corap's Ninth French Army sector. German panzer divisions now threatened the right rear of the BEF, a threat which Gort temporarily countered by the creation of Petreforce in Arras and Macforce, which at the time was thinly spaced along the Haute Deûle and Scarpe Canals. Despite this, German commanders were quite rightly concerned that an Allied counterstroke from both north and south of the River Somme could in effect turn the tables on the German advance, cut off their supply lines and trap them on the Channel coast.

Frankforce

Under the command of Major General Harold Franklyn, who commanded the 5th Division, Frankforce was formed on 20 May (the same day that German forces reached the channel coast). In addition to the six battalions of the 5th Division, Frankforce drew in two brigades of the 50th Division and 1 Tank Brigade, together with the units of Petreforce now established in Arras.

Although it was fast becoming clear that the BEF was now cut off from French forces in the south, Gort still firmly believed that the gap in General André Corap's Ninth French Army sector must be closed if disaster was to be prevented. But, as he later explained to General Edmund Ironside, this was an undertaking that the French had to initiate from the south, as all the BEF's divisions – except two, which

Chief of the Imperial General Staff , General Sir Edmund Ironside.

were at Arras with Frankforce – were committed to defending the line of the Escaut. Ironside, as Chief of the Imperial General Staff, had been sent by Churchill and the War Cabinet to appraise the situation and pressure Gort into attacking south in conjunction with the French.

From the relative security of the cabinet office in London the plan seemed eminently sensible; and despite Gort's scepticism, the 5th and 50th Divisions were earmarked to support any allied attempt to attack towards Amiens. As history records, Gort remained faithful to supporting General Alphonse Georges' assertion that the 3rd Army Group, under the command of General Antoine-Marie-Benoît Besson, was being assembled in the south. Gort may well have remained personally unconvinced that the French would attack from the south to close the gap; but it would appear that the intended Frankforce attack of 21 May was planned with a view to advancing alongside the French in order to cut off German lines of communication. We are told that on 19

General Alphonse Georges, seen here in conversation with Lord Gort.

May General Gaston-Henri Bilotte, commanding the First Army Group, had told General Georges, who was commander in chief of the northeast front, during a telephone conversation that the British intended to evacuate and return to England. This may well have been on Gort's mind but, at this point in the campaign, the British commander in chief was still intent on salvaging some sort of victory out of the chaos that surrounded him.

This rather negates the notion that the Arras counterstroke was designed as a 'stand alone' offensive and supports the more widely held assumption that the British and French attack on 21 May was intended

6

as part of a major assault on the so-called Panzer 'corridor' that had been created by Army Group A. It is possible that Gort saw the attack as an opportunity for decisive action rather than the inconclusive defence and retreat that the BEF had become embroiled in so far. It also adds to the weight of evidence that supports the view that the British did not plan to desert their French allies *before* the decision to evacuate via Dunkerque was finally announced on 26 May.

Ironside's intervention

Having been appraised of the reality of the situation on the ground by Gort, and learning that Gort had received no orders from Billotte for days, Ironside took Lieutenant General Henry Pownall, Chief of the General Staff for the BEF, with him and visited the 65-year-old Billotte at his HQ at Lens on 20 May. Informing him of the intended Frankforce attack planned for 21 May, Ironside was not impressed with what he found. Convinced that a co-ordinated Allied attack could break the encirclement around the French First Army Group, both he and Gort realised action was needed immediately if there was to be any chance that defeat was to be turned into victory. To be fair, this was a view shared by Gamelin, who had issued Instruction No.12 on 19 May, pointing out the 'vacuum' behind the German first echelon. His replacement that evening saw Weygand temporarily cancelling the instruction before settling down to what he described as some much needed sleep.

Billotte agreed to support the British operation with an attack by two divisions from General René-Félix Altmayer's V Corps towards Cambrai. Whether this was before or after the visit from the imposing six foot four inches tall 'Tiny' Ironside is a matter of conjecture. Apparently Ironside shook the demoralized Billotte by a button on his tunic. Having made Weygand aware of his conversation with Billotte, Ironside complained bitterly that both Billotte and Blanchard appeared to be completely discouraged and undecided, writing in his diary, 'no plan, no thought of any plan, just ready to be slaughtered'.

The British counterstroke

As far as Harold Franklyn was concerned, he was adamant that he was given no indication by Gort of the 'wider' picture and therefore, presumably, had no knowledge of the British War Cabinet's orders for the BEF to break the German encircling movement by attacking south towards Amiens! Franklyn writes that he was under the impression that he was about to undertake an attack of limited importance to relieve the Arras garrison and cut off German lines of communication by securing the approach roads to the south.

To the best of my memory he [Gort] used the term mopping up. I certainly got the impression that I was only likely to encounter weak German detachments ... I am still unable to understand why he painted such a distorted picture. At the time there were seven German armoured divisions operating between Arras and the River Somme twenty miles further south, rather a tall order for me to mop up.

It took a more down to earth assessment from Herbert Lumsden of the 12/Lancers, whose Morris armoured cars had spotted the 8th Panzer Division near Beaumetz-les-Loges and the 5th Panzer Division on the Cambrai road. 'Lumsden painted a very different picture of the opposition I was likely to encounter south of Arras', leaving little doubt in Franklyn's mind that his task was going to be 'far more difficult than one of mopping up'.

The most immediate question that springs to mind is why Gort did not give Franklyn fresh orders in the light of what was known about the strength of German opposition? Franklyn already knew a larger offensive strike had been planned, as he had previously met Altmayer, the commander of the French V Corps, who had asked for British co-operation, a request that Franklyn declined as he 'had received no orders to do so'. It does leave one wondering why Franklyn did not seek further clarification from Gort.

It is interesting that Martel, commanding the 50th Division, in his initial briefing on 21 May to the commander of the tank brigade, Brigadier Douglas Pratt, and the two Chief Royal Artillery officers (CRA) of the 5th and 50th Divisions, made light of the opposition they were about to face. Whether this was intentional on the part of Martel or possibly because Franklyn had not passed on Lumsden's intelligence is unclear, but it was symptomatic of a very hurried operation thrown together at the last moment. It was only during his later visit to Billotte's HQ, which he undertook with Major General Martel, that Franklyn began to realize that the Frankforce attack planned for 21 May was being seen by GHQ as a preliminary move in the proposed attempt to close the gap.

Brigadier Douglas Pratt commanded the 1ˢᵗ Army Tank Brigade at Arras.

Late on 20 May it was announced that the French support would not be ready in time to take part in the attack, a notion that appeared not to concern Franklyn, as he was still acting under his initial orders and saw no reason to delay the limited tasks he had been given by Gort. In the event, the Frankforce attack was supported by sixty tanks of the French 3rd Light Mechanized Division (3/DLM) from General René Prioux's Cavalry Corps and by the 12th Lancers, who were also covering the right flank of the attack.

German dispositions on 20 May

Although the weight of the German thrust was still pushing westwards towards the Channel coast, the encirclement of Arras was almost complete as the German advance closed up in the Arras area. By late on 20 May, the 7th Panzer Division, under the command of *Generalmajor* Erwin Rommel, was to the south of Arras; it included the 25th Panzer Regiment, the 6th and 7th Rifle Regiments, which were made up of three rifle regiments each, and the 78th Artillery Regiment (AR 78). The division had only one tank regiment instead of the normal two, although the 25th Panzer Regiment had three battalions instead of two. Rommel also benefitted from the armoured 37th Panzer Reconnaissance Battalion. At the time of the Arras counterstroke, Rommel's division is thought to have had some 218 tanks, of which just over half were Czech built 38(t)s.

Generalmajor **Erwin Rommel had already made a name for himself during the 7th Panzer Division's advance from the Meuse.**

The 8th Panzer Division was commanded by *Generalleutnant* Adolf-Friedrich Kuntzen. Divisional units included the 10th Panzer Regiment, 8th Panzer Grenadier Regiment, 28th Panzer Grenadier Regiment, 8th Motorcycle Battalion, and the 59th Panzer Reconnaissance Battalion. In May 1940 the division was equipped with Czech 38(t) and Panzer Mark II and Mark IV tanks; although by the time the division engaged the Tyneside Scottish on 20 May they may have had a smaller number of tanks, due to

Generalleutnant **Adolf-Friedrich Kuntzen, seen here on the left, commanded the 8th Panzer Division.**

9

the heavy losses incurred in the Battles of the Meuse Crossings. Unbeknown to Franklyn, 70 Brigade had already been overrun by the 8th Panzer Division on 20 May as it advanced towards Hesdin.

The 5th Panzer Division, commanded by *General der Panzertruppe* Max von Hartlieb-Walsporn, was one of the earliest tank units to come into service with the Wehrmacht and was approaching the Scarpe, east of the city, on Rommel's right flank, in preparation for crossing the river and advancing north and north west. The division included the 15th and 31st Panzer Regiments, equipped mainly with Panzer Is and IIs, although it is thought the division had three Panzer IIIs and nine Panzer IVs. The two rifle regiments, of which the 13th Rifle Regiment was equipped with half track armoured vehicles and was usually committed to battle with the Panzer regiments, were supported by the 16th Artillery

Generalleutnant Joachim Lemelsen took command of the 5th Panzer Division on 22 May 1940.

Battalion. On 20 May the division was under the command of the 20th Motorized Division, which may well have been the result of a loss of confidence in Hartlieb-Walsporn's leadership after two previous 'failures' at Le Quesnoy and Mormal. This is a notion supported by the appointment of *General der Panzertruppe* Joachim Lemelsen on 22 May, taking over command of the division six day later.

Further to the west of Arras, the motorised SS-*Totenkopf* Division had arrived on the left of Rommel's panzers. The *SS-Totenkopf* Division was formed in October 1939 from concentration camp guards of the 1st (*Oberbayern*), 2nd (*Brandenburg*) and 3rd (*Thüringen*) *Standarten* Regiments of the *SS-Totenkopfverbände,* and soldiers from the *SS-Heimwehr Danzig*. In May

SS-Obergruppenführer Theodor Eicke, the commander of the SS-Totenkopf Division.

1940 the division was commanded by *SS-Obergruppenführer* Theodor Eicke and initially held in reserve during the Battle of France and invasion of the Low Countries. However, on 16 May it saw action in Belgium, where it suffered heavy casualties before arriving in the Arras area three days later.

Chapter Two

The Demise of 70 Brigade

By the end of April 1940 the BEF had increased its strength to ten divisions, a force that had been augmented by the departure from England of three incomplete Territorial divisions – 12th (Eastern), 23rd (Northumbrian) and 46th (North Midland) – to ease manpower shortages. Neither equipped for a combat role or fully trained, it was the intention to use these divisions as pioneers in constructing marshalling yards, airfields and depots. Since there was no question of using such untrained units for fighting, it was stipulated that in each brigade one battalion should undertake training while the other two laboured.

The 23rd Division

The division was a second line Territorial formation and a duplicate of the 50th Division, which consisted of only two brigades, instead of the normal three, and completely lacked any artillery or signals support. In command was the elderly 60-year-old Major General William Herbert, a former Northumberland Fusilier, who had been recalled from the reserve. Herbert had fought in the previous war, being awarded the DSO for capturing an enemy position together with fifty-nine prisoners and was awarded a bar to his DSO in January 1919. [On 15 June 1940 the 23rd Division was amalgamated with the 50th Division.] Commanding 69 Brigade was Brigadier

Major General William Herbert, from a painting by Ronald Eves.

Richard Dawnay, 10th Viscount Downe, and in command of 70 Brigade was Brigadier Phillip Kirkup, a man who was no stranger to warfare. A former commanding officer of the 8th Battalion Durham Light Infantry (8/DLI) in 1918, he concluded his war with the DSO and bar and MC.

As far as military training was concerned there was little evidence – apart from their khaki uniforms – to suggest that these eager Territorials had been allowed more than a day or two each week to become familiar with their new trade. Each man had a rifle and bayonet, but heavier weapons, such as Bren guns and the Boys Anti-Tank Rifle, were not only in short supply but had not even been fired in practice by the majority. It was a situation that prompted General 'Tiny' Ironside to seek an assurance from Gort that the so-called 'digging divisions' would not be deployed in an operational role until they had at least been issued with their full entitlement of equipment. But like many assurances in this campaign, events were quickly overtaken by circumstances.

The Canal du Nord

On 17 May the 23rd Division's war began when they were moved to take up new positions south of Arleux along the line of the Canal du Nord. The commanding officer of the 1st Battalion Tyneside Scottish (1/Tyneside Scottish), in 70 Brigade, found his force of 660 officers and men was responsible for defending some ten miles of canal. His men who, apart from their personal weapon, were armed with fourteen Bren guns, a few 2-inch mortars and half a dozen Boys rifles, were hardly in a position to stop German armour. Here, C Company from 10th Battalion Durham Light Infantry (10/DLI), were deployed as reinforcements under 1/Tyneside

Brigadier Phillip Kirkup.

Scottish command. Fortunately, before the arrival of the enemy, the Tynesiders were withdrawn on 19 May and briefly placed in reserve at Hendecourt. Almost immediately new orders were received, sending them further north to take up positions at Thélus and then along the La Bassée Canal. But events were moving fast and, at Monchy-le-Preux, their orders were changed yet again, redirecting 70 Brigade to Saulty via Beaumetz, where they were to establish contact with 36 Brigade on the Arras-Doullens road. In the space of a matter of days, the three under strength and, for the most part untrained, battalions had been miraculously transformed from pioneers to front line fighting troops, and were about to encounter the almost unstoppable might of the 8th Panzer Division. The three battalions of Kircup's brigade were organised as follows:

1st Battalion Tyneside Scottish (Black Watch)

A duplicate battalion of the 9th Battalion, Durham Light Infantry(9/DLI), which was formed in 1939 as the 12th Battalion, Durham Light Infantry

(12/DLI). The unit was very much aware of its history in the First World War, where it fought as part of the 34th Division on the Somme in 1916 and immediately sought the affiliation with a Scottish unit; becoming the 1st Battalion Tyneside Scottish, Black Watch (Royal Highland Regiment). In command was Lieutenant Colonel Hugh Swinburne, with Major Ronald Wilby as second in command. Captain Hilton Maugham commanded A Company and B Company was under the command of Captain John Dempster. Captain George Harker commanded C Company and D Company was in the capable hands of Captain Esmond Adams. HQ Company was in the charge of Captain Frank Murphy. The

Lieutenant Colonel Hugh Swinburne.

battalion arrived in France on 23 April 1940 and proceeded to Beauvoir, where it was deployed on airfield construction duties.

10th Battalion, Durham Light Infantry
Lieutenant Colonel David Marley took command of the battalion in August 1939. Major Frederick Hall was second in command, with Captain Charles McCoy in command of HQ Company. The remaining company commanders were: A Company, Captain Ian Stock, B Company, Captain George Robinson, C Company, Captain John Kipling and D Company, Captain Martin Morrison.

11th Battalion, Durham Light Infantry
The battalion was under the command of Lieutenant Colonel John Bramwell, who had as his second in command Major Charles Gee. A Company was commanded by Captain John Welford, B Company was temporarily commanded by Second Lieutenant Edward Moscrop and C Company by Captain Rupert Blackett. Captain Francis Martin commanded D Company and HQ Company were under the command of Captain Cyril Winter.

70 Brigade on 20 May 1940
As Saulty was a further twenty miles away, Brigadier Kirkup ordered that the brigade should rest up in the Neuville-Vitasse area for the night before continuing onto Saulty on 20 May. He must have known that his men were in no fit state to reply with any effectiveness to an enemy attack and his orders for the brigade transport to 'ferry' the men in stages to Saulty on 20 May would provide, at least in part, some respite from the endless

exhaustion of marching. In the early hours of 20 May the men of the 70 Brigade battalions began arriving in their respective villages and for a few hours managed to get some much needed sleep. Thus as dawn broke on 20 May 1/Tyneside Scottish were at Neuville-Vitasse, together with C Company, 10/DLI, who were still under Swinburne's command. Those officers and men of 10/DLI who had not already been transported to Lattre-St-Quentin were at Mercatel and the remaining officers and men of 11th Battalion, Durham Light Infantry (11/DLI) were split between Ficheux, Thélus and Wancourt.

The advance towards Saulty
Hugh Swinburne, prior to taking command of the Tyneside Scottish, had been second-in-command of the 9/DLI. Evidence suggests that he was a man who did not suffer fools gladly and defined a fool as anyone who failed to live up to his expectations. His account of the battle – which was probably written post war – conflicts with the 'official version' submitted by Captain John Burr as part of the war diary. It should be added the Captain Burr had been dispatched to Saulty with a billeting party on arrival at Neuville-Vitasse and was not present with the battalion during its encounter with the 8th Panzer Division. Burr's account contains numerous corrections and additions in Swinburne's handwriting, one of which openly criticises the length of time that the Transport Officer, Second Lieutenant James Dunn, and the battalion transport took during the return journey from Saulty. Swinburne writes they left at 3.00am and did not return from the thirty mile round trip until 9.00am that morning, citing this as a principle cause of the battalion's misfortune. Before the battalion left Neuville-Vitasse, Sergeant Perkins and some 140 mixed personnel from the Royal Army Ordnance Corps (RAOC) and Auxiliary Military Pioneer Corps (AMPC) were taken under command.

The battalion left the village at 7.00am on 20 May, moving tactically and leap-frogging by companies, keeping 400 yards between companies and 100 yards between individual platoons. The last company to move were C Company, who remained in position until D Company had passed through. Leading the advance were A and B Companies; A Company were ordered to march to Mercatel and hold the village until C Company had passed through them. B Company and Major Wilby were detailed to march the three miles to the road junction near the railway line and hold the position until A Company had passed through. A short time after B Company had arrived at the road junction with the D919, Lieutenant Colonel Swinburne and Battalion HQ arrived in time to greet the arrival of the battalion transport, which had just returned from Saulty. It was now 9.00am.

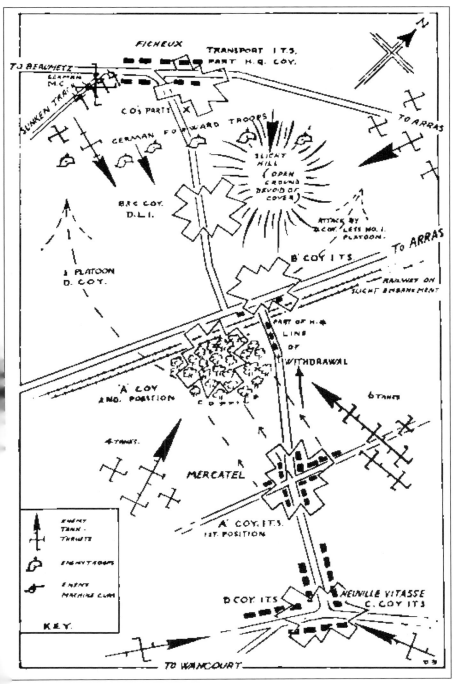

A map taken from *Harder than Hammers* depicting the route taken by 70 Brigade on 20 May 1940.

The house belonging to the Cagin family, where Second Lieutenant Robert Stordy held the turning to Ficheux.

Loading half of HQ Company, the RAOC and AMPC onto the vehicles, Swinburne instructed Second Lieutenant James Dunn to continue through Ficheux to Saulty. Before they left, Second Lieutenant Robert Stordy was ordered to hold the right flank by the road junction to Ficheux by the private house belonging to the Mangin family. At the same time Lieutenant William McGregor was ordered to make a tactical reconnaissance of Saulty with a view to the battalion preparing an all round defence. Incredibly, McGregor arrived at Saulty intact, having got through Ficheux a matter of moments before the Germans arrived.

Leaving further instructions with Major Wilby to continue with the withdrawal, Swinburne took Second Lieutenant Clifford Cohen, the Battalion Intelligence Officer, and three other ranks with him and set off behind the transport for Brigade HQ at Barly, with the intention of reporting to Brigadier Kirkup. Turning right at the junction, Swinburne headed towards Ficheux where, at approximately 9.15am, his vehicle was fired upon from machine guns positioned in the sunken road to the left of the main road. The first burst shattered Swinburne's windscreen and killed the driver, bringing the vehicle to a halt; ahead, the transport containing part of HQ Company, the RAOC and AMPC were also under fire. Private Alex Ross was travelling in one of the vehicles when they came under fire from the 8th Motorcycle Battalion:

16

We only travelled a short distance when we came under heavy machine gun fire. Our driver was killed and the lorry left the road after it had passed the road in front of a farm where there was a stable. One of our vehicles was on fire ... I went behind the stable when all of a sudden a fire broke out. There were a number of pigs with their skin on fire who were running in all directions.

Whether or not Ross was describing Darras Farm, where the barn was on fire, is unclear, as the farmhouse at Pronier Farm had also been set alight by enemy shelling. According to André Coilliot, several of the 10/DLI were killed and wounded around the Darras Farm buildings; these men were probably those from B Company. But without doubt the farm described by Private Malcolm Armstrong was Pronier Farm, which was just over a mile from the level crossing where they had been loaded onto the transport. Armstrong remembered being in the rear of his vehicle and shouting for his mate, 39-year-old Arthur Todhunter, to get out:

He couldn't as he was already dead. There was panic everywhere. I went round to the left and saw a small tank approaching. We were given orders to fix bayonets to attack. Surprised, I noticed that the cannon turned towards me but I escaped death when he changed direction, fired and one of the other lads fell. With Private Albert Foster, who was killed later, we advanced along the side of Pronier Farm. I was going to go in when a bullet or something similar struck my rifle and I dropped it. As I bent down to pick it up I was again saved when something just missed me. I then ran to an area behind this building and saw a dozen of my comrades mown down by machine gun fire.

Lieutenant Cohen was awarded the MC for his part in the battle, the citation drawing attention to his 'exceptional devotion to duty and personal gallantry in the face of the enemy'. Cohen was the last man to be captured after the convoy had been ambushed, firing a rifle until his ammunition was exhausted. Despite these furious attempts to escape enemy tanks and infantry, many of the surviving men were taken prisoner. Swinburne was eventually captured near Avenses-le-Comte on the night of 22/23 May. However,

Lance Corporal John Saunders was taken prisoner at Ficheux and later killed at Stalag VIIIb in 1944. He is buried at Popielow Cemetery in Poland.

a tiny group of men, under the command of Second Lieutenant James Dunn, succeeded in getting some vehicles away and survived the encounter.

D Company, Tyneside Scottish

Captain Esmond Adams and D Company withdrew from Neuville-Vitasse at 8.15am and passed through C Company. While they were on the road to Mercatel firing was heard behind them and Adams remained with one platoon ready to assist C Company if required. The remaining platoons of D Company continued to the railway line where Battalion HQ was now located. Here they were reunited with Adams and his men, who had commandeered civilian cars, and reported C Company was cut off in Neuville-Vitasse. Firing was now heard from the direction of Ficheux, and Adams, suspecting the commanding officer and the battalion transport had been ambushed, set off on a borrowed bicycle to reconnoitre the ground ahead of him. On his return he sent one platoon, under the command of Second Lieutenant Ian Hunter, to advance around the left flank with the intention of working behind the enemy machine guns; while the remainder of the company moved round the right flank. Both these rather bold excursions met with failure and, after sustaining heavy casualties, D Company split up into small groups and dispersed. Whether or not Adams had run into an advanced column of the 7th Panzer Division is open to conjecture, but it is possible that a unit of Rommel's division was on the fringes of Ficheux on 20 May. In any event, Adams and Hunter were both taken prisoner.

C Company, Tyneside Scottish

George Harker's men were attacked in Neuville-Vitasse almost as soon as D Company had left the village. With German AFVs closing on both flanks, a determined but very costly defence was made in the face of overwhelming odds. But, with any escape to the rear sealed by German infantry and all ammunition expended, the surviving men were compelled to surrender. Harker and a small group managed to escape and evaded captivity for three days.

A Company, Tyneside Scottish

Captain Maugham and his company were attacked in Mercatel but managed to reach the shelter of a small coppice on the Mercatel side of the railway embankment. However, any attempt to move forward was interrupted by German AFVs from the 8th Panzer Division closing in on both flanks. 43-year-old Company Sergeant Major Charles Baggs, who had fought in the previous war with the Machine Gun Corps, recorded his impressions of the fighting.

The Tyneside Scottish had little chance of surviving an encounter with the heavily armed 8th Panzer Division.

Now Jerry was on top of us, so now for action. I could hear the Battalion in action, so I moved my second platoon forward to give what assistance I could. Owing to mortar and machine gun fire I moved in extended order up to the railway embankment overlooking Ficheux. [Moving] *into position I could see the boys fighting like hell with tanks all around them, simply going over the men, and what a terrible sight. I opened out, giving what assistance I could, and I was quite happy, controlling my men, when a German machine gun opened up, on my left flank,* [pouring] *enfilade fire on us, and did he do his stuff. He simply raked us with machine gun fire and, to complete his work, two tanks came up behind us and positioned themselves about twenty yards away. They opened up with their 2-pound shells and simply blasted us out of the embankment. We were at last surrounded and within a minute or two I had fourteen killed and sixteen wounded. To hear those lads moaning made me feel rather sick. I myself didn't feel too grand, having been hit myself in the foot. When hit, I rolled down the bank and just missed being blown to hell by a tank shell.*

19

The Boys anti-tank rifle. Although adequate against light tanks in 1940, the Boys was ineffective against heavier armoured vehicles.

As the battle became fragmented many of the Tynesiders continued fighting in the face of enormous odds. Provost Sergeant Dick Chambers was killed as he attempted to fire through the slits in a tank turret, Lance Corporal Frederick Laidler – no relation to Jim Laidler – continued to play his pipes until he was shot down and CSMs Alfred Parmenter and John Morris took over Boys anti-tank rifles after their crews had been killed until they too were overrun. Maugham gave the order to take up position in the small coppice that, in May 1940, was north of the D34. But, caught in the open, enemy tanks and infantry surrounded the lightly armed Tynesiders who, having been shelled out of the shelter of the coppice, and pushed up against the railway embankment, were forced to surrender. Maugham and Baggs were taken prisoner. Baggs and some of the wounded were loaded onto a German tank and taken down the road to Ficheux:

> *Down the road he went towards Ficheux Village and it was a very sad sight seeing our dead comrades lying all over the fields on each side of the road. What a sacrifice! We passed a barn in which was an inferno, blazing like hell, and some of our boys are inside, burnt to death. We saw at least two bodies, half in and half out of the barn door, burnt black. God what a sight! The tank stopped just on the edge of Ficheux and dumped us off among some other wounded boys.*

It is more than likely that Baggs was describing the scene at Pronier Farm, which was on fire and on the outskirts of Ficheux.

B Company, Tyneside Scottish
Captain John Dempster and B Company were on the Mercatel side of the

railway line when they heard firing coming from Ficheux. Dempster went forward and was badly wounded by enemy fire. Command may have been devolved to Second Lieutenant Alfred Dodds but, in the resulting delay, D Company were ordered to make a flanking attack, while B Company held the flanks on the railway line. They were surrounded and overrun by tanks, sustaining heavy casualties before being ordered to break up into small groups and head north. Both Dempster and Dodds were taken prisoner.

HQ Company, Tyneside Scottish
Captain Frank Murphy had only half of the company established in the two fortified building by the level crossing and road junction. These were, however, set alight by enemy shelling and the surviving men forced into the open, where they surrendered.

B and C Companies, 10 /Durham Light Infantry
Fortunately 10/DLI managed to get the bulk of A and D Companies and part of HQ Company to Lattre-St-Quentin early in the morning and Lieutenant Colonel David Marley and his men were largely unaware of the misfortune that was to take place behind them. This was not the case with B and C Companies, who came under attack in the western outskirts of Ficheux. 37-year-old Captain John Kipling and C Company, who were still technically under the command of the Tyneside Scottish, overtook B Company, which had halted on the Mercatel side of the railway line and, after a quick conference with Captain George Robinson, moved forward together. Passing through B Company of the Tyneside Scottish,

A poor image but the only surviving photograph of the British dead who were buried in Pronier Farm at Ficheux and later reinterred at Bucquoy Road British Cemetery.

they came under fire between the railway line and Ficheux and were overrun by tanks. Not a single survivor remained from C Company but the few survivors from B Company that managed to extricate themselves included Captain George Robinson and Private George Walton, who finally reached the coast on 2 June 1940. Both were captured two days later as they were launching a boat out to sea. Captain John Kipling from Spennymoor, County Durham, was killed during this engagement.

11/Durham Light Infantry
Those of 11/DLI that were still in Wancourt were attacked at 8.30am by the armour of the 7th Panzer Division and units of the *SS-Totenkopf* Division, and, in the short engagement that followed, were all either killed or captured. Included amongst this number was 46-year-old Lieutenant Colonel Bramwell, who was taken prisoner.

Aftermath
In due course the surviving men of 70 Brigade were gathered together by 43-year-old Lieutenant Colonel David Marley, commanding 10/DLI, at Lattre-St-Quentin. When the brigade finally reconvened at Houdain a few days later only 233 officers and men answered their names.

Cemeteries
Mercatel Communal Cemetery and Bucqouy Road British Cemetery are described in **Car Tour 1**. **Wancourt Communal Cemetery** is about one kilometre west of the village on the N34 – Rue d'Artois. Just before the road continues under the A1 motorway, take the left turning at a small crossroads. The cemetery is 200 yards further on. You will find the British casualties from May 1940 south of the entrance. Of the five casualties buried here, three are unidentified. 23-year-old **Private Alfred McConochie,** who served with the 10/DLI, is buried next to 21-year-old **Private William Rigby** of the 11/DLI and both men were killed on 20 May. In Wancourt Rommel's 7th Panzer Division and units of the *SS Totenkopf* Division came across two companies of 11/DLI at 8.30am, which is probably where Rigby was killed. McConochie may have been a casualty from the engagement at Mercatel. 27-year-old **Flying Officer John Graafstra** was flying a Hurricane from 242 Squadron when he was shot down on 23 May 1940. He was one of fourteen Hurricane and Spitfire losses recorded on 23 May, a day that also saw the loss of Squadron Leader Roger Bushell from 92 Squadron. Bushel came to fame as 'X' at Sagan PoW camp, from where he organised a mass escape in 1944. He and fifty other officers were murdered after recapture.

Chapter Three

Petreforce

Established on 18 May under the overall command of 48-year-old Major General Roderick Petre, the Arras garrison largely consisted of a collection of troops from the 12th and 23rd Divisions, with the addition of some GHQ units that remained in the city after Brownrigg and GHQ (Rear) had departed. Petre established his headquarters in the cellars of the Palais-St-Vaast, which had been used by British forces during the First World War. The garrison included thirteen light tanks under the command of Captain Geoffrey Cooke, about thirty other ranks from the Military Police commanded by Captain Gough and a group of about 120 other ranks – dubbed the 'Station Rifles'- which had been collected from various leave trains stranded in the railway station at Arras.

Major General Roderick Petre.

GHQ

GHQ moved in two echelons from Arras to Hazebrouck and Boulogne on 17 May. GHQ (Rear), which remained in Arras, was moved to Boulogne a day or so later on the orders of the Adjutant General, Sir Douglas Brownrigg; a move no doubt hastened by the extent of the breakthrough by the German Army Group A. But, as he was to discover, nowhere on the French north-west coast was safe from the marauding Panzer divisions.

Lloyd's Gunners

A lines of communication 'scratch' battery, consisting of eight or nine 25-pounders and two 60-pounders, was assembled from the 12th Division Reinforcement Unit and put into defensive positions where 'targets of opportunity' could be engaged over open sights. Placed under the command of 24-year-old Captain Cyril Lloyd, a general staff officer with the 12th Division who had previously served with 57/Field Regiment, the battery was used principally in an anti-tank role, firing over open sights.

General Headquarters of the BEF was based at the Palais-St-Vaast in Arras. The photograph shows the entrance to the Palais-St-Vaast on Rue Paul Doumer and the cathedral, whose entrance is on Rue des Teinturiers.

3 (Ulster) Searchlight Regiment

As GHQ troops, the officers and men from the searchlight batteries appeared to be deployed far and wide during May 1940. However, 9/Battery did construct and garrison road blocks on three roads south of Arras between 17 and 18 May before they were withdrawn to Mont-St-Eloi. 10/Battery deployed one officer and forty men from H Troop to St-Laurent-Blangy to reinforce the 9/West Yorkshires. This group was not withdrawn until 22 May. It would also appear likely that anti-aircraft batteries were already in Arras as GHQ troops to deal with the constant threat from the *Luftwaffe*. However, it is not clear which units were in the city at the time.

9/(Overseas Defence) West Yorkshires

There is no war diary for this unit and the battalion was disbanded in June 1940 on return to England. It was formed in November 1939 from lines of communication (L of C) troops and were initially deployed on airfield guard duties. On arrival in Arras, under the command of 57-year-old Lieutenant Colonel Richard Luxmoore-Ball, they were positioned to hold and guard the Citadel, although the 3 (Ulster) Searchlight Regiment war

Units from 5/Searchlight Brigade were present in Arras.

diary places some of them at St-Laurent-Blangy on 17 and 18 May.

Luxmoore-Ball began his soldiering in 1914 with the 1/Rhodesian Regiment and won a Distinguished Conduct Medal (DCM) in South West Africa. Commissioned in 1915, he rose to command the 1/Welsh Guards in 1918 and finished his war with the Distinguished Service Order. In 1939, having passed the age limit for active service, he somehow managed to get onto the General List and back into uniform. None of Luxmoore-Ball's men were below the age of thirty-five and many were veterans of the previous war; two of the oldest men were Corporal Reuben Jennings, who was 60 years old when he died of wounds and Private Gordon Smith, who was 55 years old when he was killed on 20 May. Contemporary accounts refer to the battalion strength at Arras being little more than a company and a half.

1/Welsh Guards

The Welsh Guards were one of only a handful of infantry battalions that were under GHQ command. Number 3 Company (Captain J Ashton), had already been deployed to the BEF Command Post as personal bodyguard to the commander in chief and were not present at Arras. The commanding officer, Lieutenant Colonel Felix Copland-Griffiths, arrived in Arras with the advance party early on 17 May, the remainder of the battalion arriving by lunchtime, although the battalion war diary suggests the Prince of Wales Company was in Arras as early as 14 May. The battalion Headquarters, signallers and the anti-aircraft platoon were based in the Palais-St-Vaast and HQ Company (Captain Henry Dimsdale) were deployed to the northwest of the city. No. 2 Company (Captain Jocelyn Gurney) held the southern perimeter, with 4 Platoon on the Cambrai road and 5 Platoon holding the road block on the Bapaume road. The Prince of Wales Company (Captain Sir William Makins) held a road block with 2 Platoon on the Doullens road and 1 Platoon initially manning the road block at the St-Nicolas bridge and then, later in the day, were moved to establish a road block over the railway at the north end of the station complex. The sentries for the Palais-St-Vaast were supplied by 3 Platoon. No. 4 Company (Captain Maurice Smart) held the northern approaches and the road blocks at the Ste-Catherine Bridge with 11 Platoon and the St-Nicolas Bridge with 12 Platoon. On 18 May 10 Platoon, under Platoon Sergeant Major (PSM) Jones, took over three road blocks at Achicourt.

5th Battalion Yorkshire Regiment (Green Howards)

Commanded by Lieutenant Colonel William Bush, the battalion arrived in Arras around midnight on 21/22 May. Battalion HQ was established in Palais-St-Vaast with B Company (Captain William Dumville) guarding the St Pol road and D Company (Captain Chadwick) on the Doullens road. C Company (Captain Anthony Steede) defended the approaches to the Citadel and A Company (Major William 'Will' Lacy) were deployed along the road from Achicourt and in the railway sidings on the southern edge of the city.

8/Royal Northumberland Fusiliers

Formed in 1939, the battalion was a duplicate of the 4/Motor Cycle Reconnaissance Battalion and sailed for France with the 23rd Division in April 1940. Tasked with airfield construction, the battalion was ill equipped to assume a fighting role; however, under the command of Lieutenant Colonel F B Clarke, the forward elements of the battalion arrived in Arras around 12.00pm on 20 May. Their initial deployment was along the west, east and northern perimeters; but the arrival of the

Green Howards meant that they took over the western perimeter from Captain N Nicholson and B Company. The battalion finally consolidated its positions along the eastern perimeter with A Company and Captain D Portnell; and along the northern perimeter with Captain N D Pigg and C Company. One platoon under Second Lieutenant R Wilson reinforced the bridge at St-Nicolas and another, under Second Lieutenant C H Mitchell, strengthened the garrison at Ste-Catherine's bridge.

65/(Norfolk Yeomanry) Anti Tank Regiment

Major Alan Coleman and 257/Battery arrived in Arras on 20 May, having been detached from the 50th Division to assist the Arras garrison. The four guns of C Troop (Second Lieutenant George Lockett) were sited around Palais-St-Vaast whilst those of A Troop (Troop Sergeant Major Neal) were in the north eastern sector, with one gun in the station square and another at the foot of the bridge held by the Prince of Wales Company, Welsh Guards. Two of the B Troop (TSM Smith) guns were placed on the main road running into Arras and the remaining two were placed in mobile reserve.

The twelve anti-tank guns of 257/Battery were under the command of Major Alan Coleman.

242/Field Company, Royal Engineers

Designated GHQ Troops and initially attached to Frankforce on 20 May,

27

the company were under the command of Major T E Abraham, who was ordered to deploy two sections of the company to Arras. Leaving Captain Frazer in command at Givenchy-en-Gohelle, Abraham and his advanced party arrived in the city at 10.00pm on 21 May. The next day Frazer brought the remaining men and equipment of the company into Arras, arriving at1.00pm on 22 May. Abraham's sappers were employed in cratering approach roads and laying anti-tank mines.

61/Chemical Warfare Company, Royal Engineers

Based at Lattre-St-Quentin, a few miles west of Arras, the company were active in and around the city several weeks before being attached to Petreforce. The company was one element of the 1/Chemical Warfare Group and was held in GHQ Reserve along with 58 and 62/Chemical Warfare Companies. A Chemical Warfare Company consisted of an HQ and three sections, each of three sub-sections, equipped with thirty Livens Gas Projectors and organized in such a way that it could quickly assume the more traditional role of an RE field company. The Livens Projector was a crude First World War vintage mortar, capable of throwing a thirty-pound canister some 1000 yards. The company was under the command of 35-year-old Major William Anderson, who had already distinguished himself on the NW Frontier of India with the award of the Military Cross; the award of a second MC was the result of his actions at Arras. Anderson's company were very active in

Commanding 61/Chemical Warfare Company was Major William Anderson. He is seen here on the left, standing next to Captain Van der Huvel at Colditz Castle.

demolishing bridges and laying mines to slow down the advancing enemy. When the British garrison withdrew north of the railway line, the company was largely responsible for blocking the line with abandoned trains and rolling stock.

A/E Battery, 1/Royal Horse Artillery.

In 1938 E Battery merged with A Battery to form A/E Battery prior to the formation of 1 RHA. On the outbreak of war 1/RHA – less A/E Battery, who were attached to 97/Field Regiment, were deployed with the 51st Division and fought in the rearguard action at St Valery. A/E Battery, under the command of Major Arthur 'Hammer' Mathew, after withdrawing from Belgium were ordered to report to Lieutenant Colonel Herbert Lumsden of the 12/Lancers. Lumsden used the battery to strengthen the Arras garrison with their Mark II 18-pounders. The battery was withdrawn from Arras at 6.45pm on 23 May and placed back under the command of 97/Field Regiment, which was at Neuvireuil, north east of Gavrelle.

German forces

On 20 May the leading units of the 7th Panzer Regiment were in Beaurains. Fortunately for all concerned, Rommel felt he had overstretched himself and returned to Vis-en-Artois to hurry along the remaining units of the division. It was these armoured vehicles that came under fire from the guns of A/E Battery during the late morning. All that day reconnaissance units from the 7th Panzer Division were probing the defences of Arras and coming up against the road blocks manned by the Welsh Guards. At St-Nicolas, St-Laurent-Blangy and Achicourt, the 37th Armoured Reconnaissance Battalion were driven off by the defending infantry. However, the encircling German forces continued to move into position. The 20th Motorized Division advanced between the 5th Panzer Division and the western edge of Arras, while units of the 11th Motorized Brigade probed the southern approaches to Arras. Further to the east the 12th Infantry Division were on the southern side of the Scarpe, preparing to make for Souchez in order finally to seal off Arras from the east and north.

General der Infanterie **Mauritz von Winktorin, commanding the 20**[th] **Motorized Division, seen on the left standing next to** *Generalleutnant* **Heinz Guderian.**

Life in Arras

Major General Roderick Petre based himself in the cellars beneath Palais-St-Vaast and it was here that Major Alan Coleman from 65/Anti-Tank Regiment first met him on 20 May. Accompanied by his commanding officer, Lieutenant Colonel Keith Hervey, the two men drove through the deserted streets of Arras :

> *The occasion seemed to rather resemble that uncomfortable drive to the Headmaster's Study on first arrival at school, accompanied by an indulgent but anxious parent ... After some trouble we located the grim portals of the Headmaster's house, the Palais-St-Vaast, until recently no less a spot than GHQ British Expeditionary Force. Following Keith, we plunged at high speed through cellar after cellar along passages after subterranean passages and through door after gas-tight door until at last we were ushered into the Headmaster's study itself ...General Petre, a giant of a man with the mildest manners and a most engaging smile was pleased to see us and spent five minutes of his valuable time explaining to me with the aid of an enormous map the detail of his plan for the defence of the city.*

Coleman then met 46-year-old Lieutenant Colonel Felix Copland-Griffiths, who he described as a' determined little Welshman commanding the battalion of Welsh Guards in Arras', and noted that he had a considerable grasp of exactly what was taking place and where:

> *He gave me the fullest detail of all the road blocks he was manning on the main entrances to the centre of the city and asked that each of these should, if possible, be strengthened by the cover of one of my guns.*

The main body of the Welsh Guards had arrived in Arras three days before and Battalion Headquarters was temporarily situated in a house on the corner of Rue Marcel Sembat in St-Nicolas, before moving, with the Signal and Anti-Aircraft Platoons, to Palais-St-Vaast, where it remained throughout the Guards' stay in Arras. During their journey from Izel-lès-Hameau, Corporal Eric Cole recalled with disbelief the number of refugees that were on the road and wondered how they were supposed to defend the city with all these people about:

> *There were thousands of people, a never ending stream of refugees, some pulling hand carts, others with prams, horses and*

Arras after one of the many bombing raids on the city.

carts. Young people, old people; it was a shambles; all rushing to get as far away from the enemy as possible.

On 18 May command of the garrison fell to Lieutenant Colonel Copland-Griffiths, who devolved command of the Welsh Guards to his second-in-command, Major Walter Greenacre. Unfortunately, Major General Petre failed to provide Copland-Griffiths with any staff; and took the battalion Adjutant, Captain Archibald Noel, as his principal staff officer. Greenacre was obliged to promote the Signals Officer, Lieutenant Walton 'Tony' Fogg-Elliot, to combine his signal duties with that of temporary Adjudant.

On 19 May the first of the heavy bombing raids on the city commenced, which not only destroyed the railway station but also wrought havoc amongst the civilian population, killing and wounding a large number. In No.2 Company, Guardsman Robert Parker was killed and two others wounded during one air raid. No.2 Company were coming under increased pressure from German attempts to break into the city. Lieutenant Rhidian Llewellyn and 5 Platoon, who were in positions on the Arras-Bapaume road, remembered one attack on 20 May that began with a cow being driven up the road towards them:

Station Square as it was in 1940 with the Arras Memorial on the right. The railway station buildings can be seen on the extreme right.

A single rifle shot despatched the cow before it could set off the mines. The platoon position was then attacked by six tanks. The battle raged for at least two hours. The road block was set alight and burnt furiously. The front section was blasted and burnt out of its position, as was the other section protecting platoon HQ. Both sections were withdrawn ... this left [Private] Austen Snead firing his anti-tank rifle exposed to the full onslaught of the attacking tanks' weapons, protected by no-one. He continued to fire for the next one and a half hours. The anti-tank rifle had little powers of penetration against armour, however, Austen's well aimed fire against these tanks persuaded them to disengage and withdraw, leaving a deafened anti-tank rifleman to lick his wounds and them to lick theirs.

This attack was preceded by another, this time on the 4 Platoon road block further to the north east on the N39. On this occasion a civilian car containing two men in French uniforms attempted to pass the road block. When it became clear that passage was being denied, two enemy tanks appeared, which were promptly dealt with by a 25mm anti-tank gun, forcing the crews to abandon their vehicles and take refuge in nearby houses. Lance Sergeant Douglas Griffiths and his men dislodged them after some fierce hand to hand fighting, with Griffiths personally bayoneting two of the enemy, an incident that resulted in Griffiths being awarded the MM.

Situated between these two roads defended by No.2 Company was Second Lieutenant Tony Younger and his section of sappers from 61/Chemical Warfare Company:

We were given a sector in the south-east of Arras to defend between two main roads. The 1st Battalion, Welsh Guards were in charge of the defence of probably the whole of Arras and certainly of this sector. And they had two posts, one on the main road going due east, and the other on the main road going south-east. I was asked to fill in between these two posts, covering a sector, I suppose, of about a quarter of a mile. There were several roads coming into my sector from the expected direction of attack – south-east – so the first thing I did was to get some anti-tank mines to put in the road; we had no way of stopping a German tank if one had come other than our Boys anti-tank rifle – which we didn't really expect to be able to stop too much. So I went to GHQ, and found out where to draw up mines, and then placed them in these various roads. But there was a disaster on the first night. I'd put double sentries out to make sure that no French vehicles – or British for that matter – went over these mines. Sometime in the middle of the night, I was awoken by the most appalling bang. And it turned out that a huge French civilian lorry had come along the road and refused to stop when the first sentry, Sapper Kirkbride, tried to stop him. The second sentry, Sapper Calvert, moved out in front of him to try to get him to stop – but he didn't stop. And he went over one of the mines. Sapper Calvert was standing in front of him and he was killed. Sapper Kirkbride was luckily screened by the vehicle. The vehicle was destroyed, the whole of the front of it was blown up, but the driver, who was

Second Lieutenant Tony Younger. The photograph was taken after the war.

33

very high off the ground, appeared to be alright, and just disappeared. The lorry just stayed there. We couldn't move it, and we had to lay new sentries. And there wasn't much time until we stood to at dawn.

The CWGC database records the death of 23-year-old Sapper Henry Calvert as August 1941 whilst in captivity. He is buried in the Berlin 1939-1945 War Cemetery. The only other sapper from Younger's unit that is buried in Arras is Sapper Gordon Carson, who lies in Arras Communal Cemetery.

The 20 May saw the garrison strengthened further by the guns of A/E Battery, 1/Royal Horse Artillery. Major Mathew and his battery were under orders to report to Lieutenant Colonel Lumsden at the 12/Lancers' Headquarters. But, as Mathew writes, 'the fog of war was very thick at this time' and his failure to locate Lumsden prompted his decision to report to GHQ [Arras] in order to get news of the whereabouts of the 12/Lancers. Arriving in Arras at 9.45am, he had some difficulty in locating Copland-Griffiths, who was eventually found in the cellars beneath Palais-St-Vaast:

The Battery Commander [Mathew] asked for news of the 12/Lancers which no one could give. After explaining his orders to General Petre, he was directed that the battery should come temporarily under his command and should move north of the river [Scarpe] and should get into action as soon as possible, bringing fire to bear on the road Arras-Cambrai, along which the enemy were reported to be advancing. He [Petre] said that German tanks were at that moment attacking from the south [of Arras] and that speed was essential. The Battery commander returned to the battery and ordered [the] immediate move.

Coming into action near Anzin-St-Aubin, Mathew 'bumped' into an armoured car from the 12/Lancers en-route to Amiens who indicated that the 12/Lancers were now at Roclincourt and he was expected to report there. Meanwhile, the battery was firing on a number of German armoured vehicles that were advancing along the Arras-Cambrai road. The war diary reported '30 to 40 light tanks and some armoured cars were seen and engaged. More tanks, number not estimated, were seen moving off the road and south of it'. It is likely these vehicles were part of Rommel's 7th Panzer Division. While this engagement was in process Lumsden ordered the battery to support the Arras Garrison and relocate to Écurie, where they arrived at 10.00pm after an exhausting day of constant fire and movement. Establishing an observation point (OP) in a water tower at Arras, the battery remained at Écurie until 23 May.

Having been released from the 'Headmaster's Study', Major Alan Coleman and the 257/Battery guns took up positions at the key points in Arras as indicated by Copland-Griffiths. Unlike those who were already *au fait* with German air attacks and had learned to take cover quickly, Coleman still had much to learn about urban bombing attacks:

Lieutenant Colonel Herbert Lumsden commanded the 12/Lancers.

I noticed the whole of the large square, approximately the size of Piccadilly, seemed curiously deserted. Chancing to look upwards I soon saw the reason. An ugly looking packet of twelve dive bombers had approached unobserved [by me] *and the first three were just in the middle of their dive – their target being apparently Piccadilly. Normally the dive bomber gives very reasonable warning: you can see him circle his target with circumspection, then the leader gives a wicked little rock with his wings and leads the first three down with him in a good steep dive, making an awe inspiring whine with his engine, before releasing his bombs ... Normally, therefore, if you have a funk hole handy, you can conveniently wait till the machines are well into their dive before you pop as gracefully as you can under cover. In this case however, I had forgotten how deaf you are on a motorcycle and had ridden into trouble properly.*

Escaping death by the skin of his teeth, in what was probably the Place des Héros, Coleman remarked in his diary that from then on he did the 'most religious and continuous neck exercises' whenever he found himself on a motorcycle in daylight.

Regardless of Major Coleman's adventures, bombing casualties became much heavier, the Welsh Guards reporting that No.4 Company had two bombs dropped on the billets of 12 Platoon, killing six men and wounding nine others. During the same raid, HQ Company saw thirteen of its men killed and several others wounded when three bombs fell onto an air raid shelter. Fortunately the Battalion Butcher, Guardsman Benjamin, who was almost blown from the doorway, suffered only a bump to his nose!

On 21 May Copeland-Griffiths withdrew the garrison north of the railway line, leaving Major William Anderson, commanding 61/Chemical

It was an air raid by a flight of Junkers 87b Stukas that surprised Major Alan Coleman in the Place des Héros.

Warfare Company, to oversee the blocking of the line with rolling stock and railway engines. The bridge at the north end of the station was blown and the railway lines converted into an impenetrable tank obstacle by piling railway engines and rolling stock together. Engines with open throttles were driven into each other until the whole area became a solid jumble of smashed rolling stock. Behind this obstacle the British garrison took up new positions in the buildings bordering the station square.

The arrival of the 8/Northumberland Fusiliers on 20 May, along with the 5/Green Howards a day later, at least signified Gort's intention to hold onto Arras for as long as possible. Intent on maintaining an escape corridor to the north, Lieutenant Colonel Clarke deployed one platoon from C Company, 8/Northumberland Fusiliers, under Second Lieutenant R Wilson, to reinforce the bridge at St-Nicolas and another, under Second Lieutenant C H Mitchell, to strengthen the garrison holding the bridge at Ste-Catherine. Major William 'Will' Lacy and A Company, Green Howards, were ordered to defend the Achicourt road near the Citadel and the railway sidings at the present day Gare de Marchandises. Lacy was an individual who typified the Green Howard's motto – *Forward Regardless*. Seemingly without fear, he embarked on his first fighting patrol armed with only a walking stick and captured a German officer, who, after being relieved of his pistol, was taken prisoner. Lacy kept the pistol as his personal sidearm for the remainder of the war. [He later served on Montgomery's staff in the Western Desert and was one of a small group responsible for the planning of the successful El Alamein offensive in 1942.]

Refugees passing the former Hôtel de Gare in Station Square.

The precarious existence of life in Arras was brought home to the Green Howards as they were unloading the Battalion office truck outside the entrance to the cellars at Palais-St-Vaast. Eleven men were killed or wounded by a direct hit from enemy bombing. Captain John Whittaker described the three days the battalion spent in Arras as three of the weirdest days he had yet experienced:

37

The city was in that eerie no-man's land between the civilian and military worlds. The shop windows were full of pre-war goods, but the streets were deserted. There were little signs of civilians, but there must have been several hundred in the city who, too feeble or too listless to escape, dragged out a miserable existence in the cellars. Some were, doubtless, there for loot, and some for no good at all from the British point of view, judging from the sporadic sniping after dark, and the mysterious Verey lights which went up at intervals. Bombers flew continually over the city, but only two main attacks [while the Green Howards were part of the garrison] *were made – a light one on the afternoon of May 22, and a really heavy one on the morning of May 23. Casualties were, however, few, owing to trench and cellar protection. The screaming raids, when the bombers howled over the housetops every evening at 6.00pm, failed to upset the morale of the Green Howards.*

The various war diaries of the units that garrisoned Arras during the latter half of May 1940 all make reference to the lack of available rations and the foraging expeditions carried out in the city. At the forefront of these expeditions was the Reverend Cecil Cullingford, who had been attached to the Welsh Guards in October 1939. No mention is made of him by name in the war diary but his looting raids into the abandoned shops and the NAFFI storage depot became almost legendary. There are some references to raiding the Salvation Army for cigarettes; but the HQ Company diary does acknowledge the food supply was 'somewhat relieved' by Cullingford's efforts, whom the war diary describes as the 'Padre':

The Quarter Master and the Padre took to looting, the latter being an expert thief. It was no uncommon thing to see the troops feeding off tinned lobster and crab. The bread problem was never solved and the battalion went without bread for about three weeks.

Cullingford survived the war, becoming senior chaplain to the 79th Armoured Division before being appointed Headmaster of Monmouth School in 1946. Whether the short supply of rations was limited to the Welsh Guards is unknown, but the Green Howards' historian writes that their Quartermaster had little difficulty in making the daily journey to and from La Bassée to bring up rations and supplies. Apart from the lack of rations, another difficulty was that of an uncontaminated water supply, particularly after the civilian supply was cut off. A well in Ste-Catherine was used initially until that became unsafe, forcing the Welsh Guards water carts to draw water from what is described as 'a lake in the pleasure gardens'. The lake referred to may well have been one of those that are currently situated just south of Ste-Catherine British Cemetery. Second Lieutenant Tony Younger discovered he had the main NAFFI storage depot in his sector, a huge building that contained 'tens of millions of cigarettes in large crates, plus tins of food and cases and cases of beer and spirits'. He found that the number of senior officers that turned up to inspect his defences were, in actual fact, more interested in what could be salvaged from the NAFFI depot! When ordered to evacuate Arras he asked whether he should to set fire to the depot 'but was told firmly no. The Germans must have been delighted with it'.

Constantly employed in dealing with enemy incursions were the carriers of the Welsh Guards Carrier Platoon commanded by 28-year-old Lieutenant Hon Christopher 'Dickie' Furness. As the eldest son of Viscount Furness he was not only heir to the Furness Shipping Company and a considerable fortune, but extremely well connected – in that his step mother, Thelma Furness, had been romantically connected with the Prince of Wales in the 1930s. His career with the Welsh Guards came to an abrupt end in 1935 when he was asked to resign his commission after an unfortunate affair with a brother officer's wife, circumstances that were reversed four years later when war was declared. On the night of 23 May Furness, with two carriers, was searching for a downed Luftwaffe airman. After crossing the bridge at Ste-Catherine he fired two bursts from his Bren gun in the hope of drawing fire from the fugitive. A split second later his carrier was struck by an anti-tank round wounding him

The Welsh Guards Carrier Platoon was under the command of Lieutenant Hon Christopher Furness.

and Guardsman Cyril Griffiths in the backside. The round was British and was fired from one of several 2-pounders in place on the road beyond the bridge. Lance Sergeant George Griffin described Furness standing up in his carrier and shouting: 'Who the hell fired that?' Although he makes no mention of the incident in his diary, it looks very much as though Alan Coleman was the 'Anti-Tank Major' that rather indignantly replied that Furness's trigger happy behaviour was responsible, as the British gunners thought they were about to be attacked. Needless to say, after apologies all round, Furness returned to Arras without the fugitive, leaving his

Each infantry battalion was equipped with the Carden Loyd Carrier. It was carriers such as these that Furness used to great effect in Arras.

disabled carrier behind. The HQ Company war diary recorded the incident:

> *He* [Furness] *was wounded and his carrier put out of action. The crew of his carrier came back in another carrier and Dick came into our mess where Buckland* [Lieutenant Quartermaster] *as usual was only too willing to help in bandaging him up.*

On another occasion Furness was riding in Lance Sergeant Sullivan's carrier and ordered Sergeant Mabey to meet him, with the remaining five carriers, in the station square:

> *As they drew up, a reconnaissance plane flew low over them, deciding Sergeant Mabey to move to a less exposed position. The end of the line* [of carriers] *had not left the square when three ME109s dived upon them and chased them down the streets, the bullets ricocheting off the houses above their heads.*

German pressure from the west increased considerably during 23 May. The western barricades were repeatedly bombed and attacked by ground troops; although they were driven off by the defending garrison, it was realised that it was only a matter of time before the weight of German armour would overwhelm and capture the city. At 6.45pm A/E Battery was withdrawn and returned to 97/Field Regiment shortly before orders arrived to hold Arras to the last round and last man. Resigned to their fate, the garrison blocked the northern exits to Arras and prepared to fight. Throughout the evening reports flooded into Palais-St-Vaast indicating German armour was pushing round the right flank and had reached Lens which, according to Gort's despatch, was the reason behind the evacuation of Arras. At 10.00pm Franklyn contacted GHQ, warning Brigadier Oliver Leese, the Deputy Chief of Staff, that unless the garrison withdrew during the night a subsequent withdrawal would be well nigh impossible; he was informed that orders for the withdrawal had been issued an hour before and were being brought by a liaison officer. As Blaxland points out, it seemed odd that these vital orders were sent by hand, which was, presumably, thought to be safer than using the telephone? In the event, it was the telephone that alerted Franklyn to the new orders. The staff officer charged with relaying the orders to Arras was Captain Charles 'Frank' Hutchinson. His failure to reach Major General Petre in Palais-St-Vaast leaves one to wonder exactly what would have taken place if Franklyn had not phoned GHQ:

Brigadier Oliver Leese later commanded the Eighth Army in the Italian campaign throughout most of 1944.

> *We drove down* [from Vimy] *in a Humber snipe car and just short of Arras we saw a German tank on the other side of the road, he saw me just a little afterwards, so we abandoned ship, got in a ditch, and crawled down to the outskirts of Arras. We heard some Geordies talking and recognized a battalion of the Northumberland Fusiliers, I shouted out 'I'm a British Officer', and that brought me under heavy Bren fire ... eventually we got near some Germans and we had to give it up, walk back around the tanks and start walking back to Vimy.*

The evacuation

The Official History tells us that orders reached units in Arras a little before midnight on 23 May; but Tony Younger and his section of sappers had already been redeployed to La Bassée Canal to blow the bridges. From Younger's account it would seem that they left Arras sometime after Copland-Griffiths had withdrawn the garrison north of the railway line on 20 May. Their sudden orders to leave took them past the railway station:

> *It did not take long to pack up, nobody wanted to hang about and, with an air-raid in progress, we drove, well spaced out, passing the main square in front of the station. Civilian casualties were everywhere. I led and had to stop where a fallen house largely blocked the road. Our sappers worked fast to open up a way through and, as I climbed back into my truck, I saw a man carrying a young girl along the pavement next to us. The expression of utter horror on his face has stayed with me to this day, and it was only when I looked down and saw the girl had no head that I realized why.*

Alan Coleman in his diary writes that he was summoned to an urgent conference in the 'Headmaster's Study' at 11.00pm on 23 May, where the orders to evacuate Arras via the St-Nicolas Bridge to Douai were relayed to commanding officers. As Coleman wrote afterwards, it was news that suited him well. 'The idea of being left to history as the heroic defenders of Arras seemed good enough for the novels of Buchan, but its attractions to me at that particular time was largely theoretical.' Then came the news that the evacuation had been cancelled and they were to fight to the last man. His obvious disappointment is displayed in his diary entry:

> *So this, I thought, is what it is like to be a nameless hero. If only I was a regular soldier I should doubtless have been filled with an inward elation that a great chance had been given to me. I walked less briskly and told them [his officers and men] the whole show was off again once more ... But not for long. At 1.30am I was roused by an orderly for yet one more urgent conference with the Headmaster.*

On this occasion Petre passed on the fresh orders to evacuate, commenting that he could not pretend that the garrison stood much chance of getting out. Franklyn was equally annoyed:

It would have been a great help if Gort's staff had given me some inkling by telephone of the change of plan and so given me an hour or more in which to extricate my force. I suppose that they were influenced by the feeling that secrecy was paramount, but in this case it should have been obvious that urgency was much more important.

Instructions to 'wake up, get up, pack up' from Copeland-Griffiths brought the Welsh Guards to a state of readiness, but it was still 3.15am on 24 May before the battalion was ready to move off. Soon after leaving St-Laurent-Blangy the road forks, with the Douai road continuing to the left and a minor road on the right following the left bank of the Scarpe. Both roads crossed the railway line, the main road to Douai over a viaduct, which had been demolished, and the minor road under a bridge, which was intact. It is thought the viaduct had been destroyed as a result of enemy bombing. Sending word to the Green Howards, who were following, to use a more westerly route via Bailleul-Sir-Berthoult, Lieutenant Colonel Bush continued over the rubble of the viaduct and headed for Gavrelle. It is thought the remaining units in Arras left the city using the Hénin-Liétard road. (the village was amalgamated with Hénin-Beaumont in 1971.) However, the Green Howards' battalion transport had headed east along the D42 and blundered into a dawn crossing of the Scarpe by IR89.

The thick ground mist probably aided the Welsh Guards as they moved out of Arras towards Douai. Most of the companies travelled independently and got away by using side roads but the transport, under the Quartermaster, followed the Green Howards along the Scarpe. The vehicles were about three miles from Arras when they ran into heavy firing from German troops. By the time Furness arrived at the St-Laurent-Blangy road junction, the traffic was still being directed to the right under the railway bridge, although it had quickly became apparent to all that this road was also under fire and traffic was in the process of turning round. It was at this point that the light tanks – presumably from Cooke's detachment– went forward to deal with the enemy while the convoy turned around; with them was Furness and three carriers.

After passing under the bridge, Furness followed the light tanks uphill as they turned off the road to the left. Climbing steadily towards the Douai road, they passed through a detachment of RNF before they headed on towards the next ridge. The area is now under the D950 road complex but Sergeant George Griffin remembered it vividly:

On mounting the ridge we could see there was a German strong

The Mark VI Light Tank.

post on the crest. Mr Furness bore to the right so as to take the position in the flank. As we approached the top, Griffiths, my driver, said 'I'm wounded'. I looked at him and he seemed so casual that I asked him if he would carry on, he said 'yes' but could only use his left arm. I had followed Mr Furness and on bearing round to the left behind the post, I saw one of the tanks with Mr Furness's carrier close beside it. Griffiths could hardly control the machine by this time, and it continued in a circle down the ridge and back again. I kept firing whenever we were facing the right way. We came round to the post a second time, and this time managed to stop close to Mr Furness's carrier. Griffiths was again hit, this time in the thigh. I saw Mr Furness stand up in his carrier grappling with a German over the side. Mr Furness shot him with his revolver and he fell to the ground. Fire was very hot indeed by this time, pinging on the plates, it was suicide to stand up.

With Griffiths getting weaker by the moment he was unable to prevent his carrier crashing into the back of Furness's vehicle and stalling the engine. Eventually, after several efforts, the engine burst into life again: *There was no sign of life either in the tank or in Mr Furness's carrier, bar the Germans squirming on the ground that he had shot, so we carried on round the back of the post. The windows were all misted over by this time, and it was difficult to see, but we managed to dodge their wire and some tank traps they had dug, and got back on the road at the bottom of the ridge'.*

It had been a costly episode but without it the Welsh Guards transport would have been unable to escape Arras. Of the three carriers that went into action there were no survivors from Furness's vehicle, who were all killed, along with 22-year-old Guardsman David Williams. Four others were wounded and Lance Sergeant Hall was taken prisoner. Furness was awarded a posthumous VC, which was announced after the war. Apart from Cyril Griffiths, who was mentioned in despatches, none of the others involved appear to have been recommended for an award despite their apparent gallantry under fire. According to the 8/RNF war diary, one light tank survived the encounter; the other two were seen to be on fire. Their war diary also records the capture of Lieutenant Colonel Clarke and the Adjutant, Major Seth-Smith, who, as a second lieutenant in 1918, had flown as an observer with the Royal Flying Corps.

Lieutenant George Lockett and C Troop led Major Coleman and the 257/Battery convoy out of Arras, but it was 4.00pm before he was clear of the city. Reaching the fork in the road at St-Laurent-Blangy, Coleman writes that he was alarmed to meet George coming back up the road towards him :

The bridge is blown up' he says 'try the other road'. This looks bad, but by a stroke of luck we are able to turn the vehicles in a broad stretch of road and get in behind the returning troop, and chance on a short cut, which after crossing a bit of hard plough-land, lets us back into the Hénin-Liétard road.

At some point Coleman became separated from his second in command, Lieutenant John Taunton, and, unsure whether he was ahead or behind him, Coleman reached Hénin-Liétard at 7.00am. A mile or so outside Douai, Coleman writes that he came across a car parked at the side of the road containing his 'late Headmaster' [Petre]:

I reported my arrival and he seemed quite pleased to see me but had no ideas as to anything I should do and recommended I go and lie up in Leforest, a village five miles back. 'Are we going to hold the line of the Deûle?' I enquired. He thought it most unlikely and reckoned we were all about due for a breather, which seemed OK by me. A mile further on I came across [Lieutenant] John Taunton asleep at the head of his little convoy of two troops, drawn up under the trees. He had got through with no trouble at all and had been there since 6.30am, having followed the same route as I had.

Cemeteries

Arras Communal Cemetery is in the St-Sauveur district on the eastern edge of the city. This is a large communal cemetery and is best accessed from the D339 Rue de Cambrai. After you pass over the girder bridge at Pont St-Sauveur near the railway station, Rue Georges Clemenceau is 750 yards further on the left. There is plenty of parking available here. The British plots are best approached using the first entrance on Rue Georges Clemenceau and following the avenue that parallels the southern wall. Just behind the French military plot and memorial you will find the British graves facing the wall. The largest plot contains twenty-seven burials, one special memorial and three which are unidentified. The fourteen Welsh Guardsman were all killed during the battalion's occupation of the city as part of Petreforce, the youngest being 21-year-

The entrance to Arras Communal Cemetery on Rue Georges Clemenceau.

old **Lance Corporal Samuel Jackson** (Y.1.57), who was one of thirteen men killed when a bomb struck their air raid shelter on 22 May. Buried close by is 23-year-old **Guardsman Peter Dinneen** (Y.I.54) from Rhydfelan, who was probably killed in the same incident. Another victim of that raid was 24-year-old **Lance Sergeant William Moore** (X.1.5). **Guardsman Robert Parker** (Y.1.63) was serving with No.2 Company when he was killed by enemy bombing on 20 May. **Guardsman Lawrence Maxwell** (X.1.25) was only 24-years-old when he was killed with six others from 12 Platoon on the night of 20 May by the bridge at Ste-Catherine. **Lieutenant Thomas Bland** (W.4.17) was mortally wounded on 21 May whilst serving

Guardsman Peter Dinneen.

with 4/Northumberland Fusiliers. He was in command of the Y Company Scout Car Platoon at the crossroads west of Beaurains, where Major Kenneth Clarke and his company held on almost to the last round before they surrendered. Bland died in captivity and the date of his death has been recorded as 30 May 1940. Like Bland, **Sapper Gordon Carson** (X.1.30) of 61/Chemical Warfare Company is buried in a single grave. He was probably killed during the final hours of the British stay in Arras on 23 May. 28-year-old **Squadron Leader Michael Peacock** and 19-year-old **Pilot Officer Richard Shrewsbury** were both shot down by ground fire on 20 May 1940 whilst flying Hurricanes from 85 Squadron. They are buried together in a joint grave. Nearby are four more aircrew from 7 Squadron, who were all killed when their Lancaster was shot down on 16 June 1944. Three of the crew survived and were taken prisoner.

Chapter Four

Frankforce – The Counterstroke

Franklyn entrusted the attack to Major General Giffard Le Quesne Martel, who commanded the 50th Division and who, as a former Royal Engineers officer with the DSO and MC, had developed a keen interest in armoured fighting vehicles as early as 1916. Advised by Brigadier Vyvyan Pope, who had transferred to the Tank Corps in 1920, his plan of attack was to advance from Vimy in two columns to the line of the Arras-Doullens road and then, using this as the start line, attack the Germans south and south-east of Arras. On paper Frankforce was composed of the two brigades of the 5th Division together with Martel's 50 Division, less 25 Brigade, which was on the La Bassée Canal, and the 1st Tank Brigade. In reality, with the 5th Division deployed on the Scarpe east and west of Arras, Franklyn only had

Major General Sir Giffard Le Quesne Martel.

the three battalions of 151 Brigade and two battalions of the tank brigade available. However, once the semi-circular attack around the south of Arras had been accomplished, it was envisaged that 13 Brigade would cross the River Scarpe and join the operation, while 17 Brigade remained in reserve. Also held in reserve was the 9/DLI, under the command of Major Joseph 'Jos' Percy, who had been appointed to the command on 11 May 1940. His battalion and the remainder of the 4/Northumberland Fusiliers were to follow the right hand column. The men of 151 Infantry Brigade were Geordies under the command of Brigadier John 'Jackie' Churchill. A former commanding officer of the 1st Battalion, Durham Light Infantry (1/DLI), Churchill was awarded the MC in 1915, finishing the war intact in the rank of major. Described as an energetic officer, he was without doubt the ideal brigade commander and one who endeared himself to officers and men alike. He would have been aware that the Durhams were already tired and footsore, having marched back from Grammont in Belgium via the La Bassée Canal, and were now being thrown into a mobile battle they had not been trained for and were in ignorance of the enemy strength and dispositions. It did not bode well.

Despite Franklyn's request for an air umbrella over Arras, it was not forthcoming and the only recorded RAF air activity was from 15 and 18 Squadron Blenheim IVs, who were tasked with attacking enemy armour in the Boulogne area. It is a sad fact that the only air umbrella on 21 May was provided by the *Luftwaffe,* who bombed and strafed British units with impunity.

German Tank Strength on 21 May

When war was declared in September 1939, the Panzer units were still in the process of training new recruits and re-equipping. By the end of September of that year, only eighty of the new Mark IIIs and 197 of the Mark IVs had been delivered to units. Tank production was in direct competition with the material requirements of the *Luftwaffe* and the growing needs of the *Kriegsmarine.* The Wehrmacht tank strength was thought to be just over 1,000 Panzer Is, 1,500 Panzer IIs and 164 Czech 38(t)s, the 7th Panzer Division being one of only three panzer divisions that were, for the most part, equipped with Czech 38(t)s. By May 1940 the number of Panzer IIIs and IVs had increased, but were well below the number demanded by the army. The Panzer I, equipped with a single machine gun, had originally been designed to provide driver training for the Panzer crews and were commonly referred to as the 'Krupps sports car'. 'Who would have thought', wrote an unhappy Guderian, 'that one

The *Panzerkampfwagen* III, commonly known as the Panzer III, was a medium tank developed in the 1930s.

day we should have to go into action with this little training tank'. It is likely that he was also unhappy with the main armament of the Panzer II, which was equipped with a 2cm gun and represented the bulk of the panzer units during the France and Flanders campaign. All of which left the Czech 38(t) Panzer IIIs and IVs as the main battle tanks.

The Left Column
The column left Vimy at11.00am and moved south past Thélus to Écurie, where it headed west through Anzin-St-Aubin and Wagonlieu to Dainville, with Hénin-sur-Cojeul as their ultimate objective, it consisted of the following units:

Generalleutnant Heinz Guderian commanded XIX Corps during the Battle of France.

4th Battalion, Royal Tank Regiment
4/RTR was under the command of Lieutenant Colonel James Fitzmaurice MC, with Major Stuart Fernie as second in command, and organized into four companies: HQ Company (Major C I Lee); A Company (Major Stuart Fernie); B Company (Captain Ivor Clement); and C Company (Major A Holford Walker). The battalion was equipped with thirty-five Mark 1 'Matilda' tanks, armed with either a .303 or a 0.5-inch machine gun, and limited to a top speed of eight miles per hour. The crew of two were almost as tightly packed as the crew of three that operated the Mark

The Infantry Tank Mark I, known as the Matilda I.

50

The Vickers-Armstrong Light Tank Mark VIb.

VIb light tanks, which at least had a top speed of 30 miles per hour. For the duration of the attack on 21 May, six Mark II 'Matilda' tanks, under the command of 47-year-old Major Gerald Hedderwick (A Company 7/RTR), were transferred to the battalion from 7/RTR. By a strange twist of fate, 4/RTR was to attack over the same ground as D Battalion of the Tank Corps on 9 April 1917.

6th Battalion Durham Light Infantry
6/DLI was a Territorial battalion in 151 Brigade and commanded by Lieutenant Colonel Harry Miller, with Major Peter Jeffreys as second in command. Its men were largely drawn from the Bishop Auckland, Barnard Castle and Spennymoor districts of Durham County and landed in France in January 1940. A Company was commanded by Captain Edward Proud, B Company by Major E Perry and C Company by Major G R Roddam. Captain Ronnie Cummins commanded D Company and HQ Company was under the command of Captain B Holroyde.

4/Royal Northumberland Fusiliers and 11 Scout Platoon
The battalion was a motor cycle reconnaissance battalion in the 50th Division under the command of Lieutenant Colonel R Wood. Major Kenneth Clark and Y Company were assigned to the column, along with the Daimler Scout cars from 11 (Scout) Platoon, commanded by Lieutenant Thomas Bland.

368 Battery, 92/Field Regiment RA

This 5th Division artillery unit consisted of two batteries of twelve guns. 368/ Battery was equipped with the more modern 25-pounders and was under the command of Major R A Martin. Although the guns teams arrived from their positions north of Givenchy in the nick of time, the support they offered was rendered almost useless as communication between the Forward Observation Officer in Beaurains' church tower and the guns broke down almost immediately. Committed to shooting off the map, the gunners failed effectively to engage the German batteries on Telegraph Hill.

206 Battery, 52/Anti-Tank Regiment RA

The 52/Anti-Tank Regiment was the senior Territorial anti-tank regiment in the British Army, which may account for it being attached to the 5th Division. Like the 65/Anti-Tank Regiment in the 50th Division, it consisted of four batteries and a headquarters. Sadly the war diary gives little away regarding the detail of the events of the day.

151 Brigade Anti-Tank Company

Lieutenant Colonel Miller is not specific in his account of whether or not he deployed the brigade anti-tanks guns at Agny and Achicourt, but we must assume that they were in action with the 6/DLI during the day.

The Right Column

On the right flank, the column had the support from elements of the French 3 DLM equipped with Somua S35 tanks and 13/Battalion Chars de Combat with their smaller Hotchkiss H35 tanks. The 12/Lancers were also operating on this flank with their CS9 armoured cars. The column left Vimy at 11.00am and proceeded through Neuville-St-Vaast, Maroeuil and Duisans, towards Boisleux-au-Mont on the River Cojeul. Contact

The French
Somua S35
Tank.

Two abandoned Hotchkiss H35 Tanks.

between the infantry and the tank column was lost at Maroeuil and the infantry never in fact arrived at the start line. The column consisted of the following units:

7th Battalion, Royal Tank Regiment

The battalion was commanded by Lieutenant Colonel Hector Heyland DSO, with Major Hugh Garrett as second in command, and like its sister battalion, was organized into four companies, which included a

The Infantry Tank Mark II, best known as the Matilda II.

The officers of the 8/DLI, taken in January 1940. Back row, fourth from left: Second Lieutenant Redfers Potts. Middle row, first left: Second Lieutenant Ian English and third left: Second Lieutenant John Leybourne. Front row, third left: Captain Walter Goodenough. Major Ross McLaren and Lieutenant Colonel Tim Beart are seated fifth and sixth from the left, while Captain Frederick Kirkup is on the end.

headquarters company: A Company (Major Gerald Hedderwick); B Company (Major John King); and C Company (Major George Parkes). The battalion was equipped with twenty-three Mark I Matilda tanks and sixteen Mark II Matildas. The Mark II had a more reasonable top speed of fifteen miles per hour and a crew of four, but most notable was the thickness of the armour plating (78mm) which was, in most cases, impervious to German anti-tank weapons.

8th Battalion, Durham Light Infantry
The 8/DLI was another 151 Brigade Territorial battalion and drew its personnel from Durham City, Chester-le-Street and Stanley. The battalion was under the command of 46-year-old Lieutenant Colonel Tim Beart MC and landed in France in January 1940, with Major Ross McLaren as second in command. HQ Company was commanded by Major John Raine, A Company was under the command of Captain John Dixon, B Company by Captain Frederick Kirkup, C Company by Captain James Walton and D Company by Captain Walter Goodenough. As with the other battalions in 151 Brigade, the battalion was a motorised unit and had its own company of Royal Army Service Corps (RASC). Yet, despite this, the men of 151 Brigade appeared to undertake an inordinate amount of marching!

4th Battalion Royal Northumberland Fusiliers
Z Company, under the command of Major J T Lisle, and 12 (Scout) Platoon of 4/Royal Northumberland Fusiliers were assigned to the column. Serving in Z Company was Captain D M Clark-Lowes, whose brother, Major Kenneth Clark, was serving in Y Company with the right column.

365 Battery, 92/Field Regiment, RA
Commanding the second battery from 92/Field Regiment was 25-year-old Major Derek Cragg-Hamilton, who was killed on 31 May near Verne. Equipped with 18-pounders, the war diary leaves little to the imagination and simply records that the battery was called upon to support the column late in the day. In actual fact it hardly got into action at all, as it failed to arrive from Givenchy until the battle was almost over, citing the huge number of refugees blocking the road. The 31-year-old Hon Thomas Roche was serving with the battery as a lieutenant in 1940 and subsequently joined the Special Operations Executive (SOE) in 1941, becoming Assistant Director of Security.

The large numbers of refugees on the roads around Arras were said to be responsible for preventing 365/Battery from giving fire support to the right hand column.

260 Battery, 65 (Norfolk Yeomanry) Anti-Tank Regiment

A single battery from this 50th Division unit, consisting of twelve 2-Pounder anti-tank guns under the command of Major Herbert Forrester, was assigned to the right hand column. The regimental war diary is brief and simply records that 260/Battery took part in offensive action west of Arras. However, it fails to mention that from their position on the Warlus ridge Forrester's guns knocked out upwards of twenty German tanks from the 25th Panzer Regiment. The battery retired to Givenchy after the battle. Forrester would later be killed in action with 3 Commando during the Vaagso Raid in 1941.

Major Herbert Forrester in conversation with King George VI just before the Vaagso Raid in 1941

151 Brigade Anti-Tank Company

At least one troop from the company accompanied Lieutenant Colonel Beart to Warlus, where they were in action against the 25th Panzer Division. There is a veiled reference made by Lieutenant John Leybourne of the Brigade gunners being at Duisans and we can only assume that one troop possibly stayed in the village with Major McLaren.

The Attack

Both columns left Vimy at 11.00am on the way to the start line on the Arras-Doullens road, where the attack was planned to begin at 2.00pm. There was apparently some confusion over the start line, with the Tank Brigade under the impression that they were to start from the line of the railway, some 700 yards south of the road. In the event it made little difference, serving only to underline the hurried nature of the preparatory briefings. In the opinion of 21-year-old Second Lieutenant Ian English, the 8/DLI Carrier Platoon commander, who had only arrived that morning, it was 'a hectic rush with very few managing to get any rest. There were few maps, no reconnaissance; orders were rushed and many went without a hot meal.' Second Lieutenant Tom Craig, a tank commander with 7/RTR, arrived at Vimy in his Matilda II tank exhausted and without time to compose himself, where he was given a map by his company commander and told to start up and follow him. 'The wireless was not working; there was no tie up with the infantry and no clear

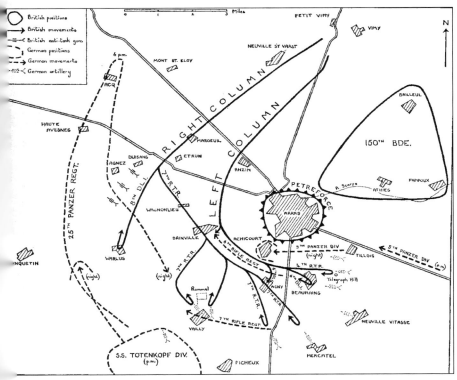

A map taken from *The Shadow of Vimy Ridge*, depicting the British and German dispositions on 21 May.

orders.' Ian English's comments mirrored those of Tom Craig, both men having concerns that the attack was going ahead before units had got to know each other, and as Ian English said later:

It was a force of all arms on paper only. There had been no combined training between tanks, infantry and artillery. Many of the DLI had never seen a tank until they were going into action with them. The left hand column had desultory and largely ineffective artillery support, and only in the later stages. The right hand column had no artillery support whatever, because the guns could not be brought near enough to the action due to the thousands of refugees blocking the roads. There were no communications between tanks and infantry due to the breakdown of R/T sets.

But English went further and highlighted the most serious misconception of all: Who exactly was in command of each column? Both infantry commanders understood the tanks were under their command while the tank commanders thought they were only in a support role, all of which eventually played into the hands of the enemy.

The Left Column
The column was the first to make contact with the enemy. Lieutenant Colonel Harry Miller, commanding the Durhams, realised early on that his men were not going to keep up with the tanks of 4/RTR. Whether he recognised this was a tactical error or not, he did know only too well from his service with tanks in 1917 that the work of armoured vehicles could quickly be undone if not followed up promptly by infantry; but first his men had a more pressing task:

I now decided it would be desirable for us to clear Agny as it occupied a prominent position overlooking the road between Achicourt and Beaurains, so I walked across and told Major Perry [B Company] to continue on that line and take in Agny and the wood northwest of it. It was very fortunate this step was taken as the bulk of our prisoners were captured in Agny. When I returned to my advanced HQ, I was met by Major [Peter] Jeffreys and he reported that touch was being lost with the tanks and suggested that we should send forward the carriers to keep in contact. I agreed to this and gave orders to go forward and prevent enemy infantry re-organizing after the tanks had passed through.

The building used by 4/RTR as Battalion Headquarters at Petit Vimy still stands today on Rue Sadi Carnot.

By now well ahead of the infantry, 4/RTR approached the level crossing on the railway line, an occasion that was not without its own drama. Second Lieutenant Peter Vaux recalled their almost embarrassing negotiation of the level crossing:

> We met trouble almost from the start because the railway cutting was a good deal steeper than we had anticipated and I remember two of the tanks went down the embankment cutting and then they couldn't get back up the other side. Then they couldn't get back the way they had come, so were stuck on the railway line. The level crossing gates were shut and there was a bell ringing, just as though a train was coming. I remember it took a good deal of effort of will before somebody was able to push on and drive clean through the gates. Then the whole regiment was over and we went, one after the other, up the hill on the other side of the railway, where we spread out.

At Achicourt the tanks of 4/RTR found the exposed flank of *Oberst* Erich von Unger's 6th Rifle Regiment. Sergeant 'Diddy' Reid was commanding a Mark 1 Matilda:

After picking up a crewman from a broken down tank, we crossed a railway line with difficulty, and this brought us under fire again. Ahead of me I saw a railway embankment and a road beyond it on which German vehicles were moving about. Everyone was firing away briskly and I claimed a side-car machine gun outfit which divided itself round a tree and a lorry.

23-year-old Second Lieutenant Peter Vaux, commanding the 4/RTR Reconnaissance Troop, almost whooped with joy as he realized they had come straight into the flank of a German mechanized column:

Second Lieutenant Peter Vaux.

They were just as surprised as we were and we were right in amongst them before they knew what was going on. For a quarter of an hour or so there was a glorious free-for-all in which we knocked out quite a lot of their lorries: there were Germans running all over the place. For the most part they were too scared to do very much but some of them had a go at jumping on our tanks and I remember that a German who climbed on the outside of mine was very kindly removed by another tank, which turned its machine gun on me and removed him.

Growing in confidence, Vaux was particularly impressed by the German gunner's inability to penetrate the armour on the Matildas. 'I don't know how many Germans we killed' he wrote afterwards, 'nor how many vehicles we destroyed', but at that moment he did not see why he should not go all the way to Berlin. Vaux and his comrades had certainly caught the Germans on the back foot:

For the most part they were too scared to do very much, but some of them had a go at jumping on our tanks and I remember that I myself had a German who climbed on the outside of my tank and looked in the periscope. I was looking out of the periscope and saw him looking in – I suppose he saw me looking out! Then a

60

neighbouring tank very kindly turned his machine gun on me and that removed my passenger.

At Dainville Y Company 4/RNF made the first ever mounted motorcycle attack, together with Captain David Hunt of C Company, when they ambushed a German column in the sunken road just south of the D59, where it passed underneath the Maroeuil-Achicourt railway line. Positioning one of his tanks by the bridge to block the route into Dainville, his tanks destroyed most of the enemy halftracks and took some forty prisoners. Today the bridge has been replaced by a level crossing.

As the tanks continued southeast towards Wancourt, elation turned to shock as two companies of tanks ran into the range of the 4th and 5th Batteries of AR 78 on Telegraph Hill. The heavier shells of the German batteries astride the wood on Telegraph Hill and the 6th Battery south of Tilloy were working together with the 88mm (8.8cm) guns north of Mercatel. It was a deadly combination, the results of which horrified Peter Vaux as he moved from the Beaurains-Tilly road towards Telegraph Hill:

The Colonel's tank was down there, a little in front of them – I could see it quite clearly, it was stationary and I could see the flag flying from it ... I went forward through those tanks of A Squadron and I thought it was very odd they weren't moving and they weren't shooting, and then I noticed that there was something even odder about them – because their guns were pointing at all angles; a lot of them had the turret hatches open and some of the crews were half in and half out of the tanks, lying wounded and dead – and I realized suddenly, with a shock, that all these twenty tanks had been knocked out and they had all been knocked out by these big guns and they were in fact, all dead – all these tanks. In the grass I could see a number of black berets as the crews were crawling through the grass and getting away, those who were not dead. Then the Adjutant came on the air and he just said, 'come over and join me.' So I motored down to the valley and as I did so I saw the Adjutant drive forward and start shooting. As I got closer I saw there were a whole number of German anti-tank guns in the area of the potato clamp and the crews were running about. I remember I owe my life to the quick-wittedness of Captain [Robert] Cracroft, because, as we got to the potato clamp, I found that there were half a dozen Germans on the other side of it. I gave orders to fire to my gunner and he was firing down into the thing but couldn't depress the gun enough, and I was standing on my

61

seat shouting at the gunner and calling to the driver to reverse a bit so we could get the bullets down low enough. I little thought that behind me was a German lying on the ground with his rifle resting on a kit bag, drawing a careful bead on the back of my neck. The Adjutant pulled out his revolver and, quick as a flash, he shot the chap in the throat.

Although Vaux had not realized it at the time, Lieutenant Colonel Fitzmaurice was dead, along with his operator 23-year-old Corporal Alan Moorhouse, as was Major Gerald Hedderwick, who had been killed on the same spot where he fought in 1917. Command was now in the hands of Major Stuart Fernie, who immediately called up his reserve C Company tanks to attack the German guns. Squadron Sergeant Major Jock Armit and his troop were amongst those who responded:

I advanced over the crest of a small ridge and ran smack into six anti-tank guns. They were not camoflaged and their only cover was a fold in the ground. My .50 MG was brought into action and before [they] realized, I was on them – the range was approximately 200 yards. The other guns started on me now and one hit the gun housing. This caused the recoil slot pin of my gun to snap and shook the gun back into the turret jamming me between the shoulder piece onto the back of the turret.

Having destroyed two of the 37mm anti-tank guns he managed to reverse his damaged tank into cover and in desperation ignited a smoke generator to provide some sort of cover, but to his horror he found the turret flap had jammed:

It was quite a shock to have the smoke generator burning in the tank with the flap jammed, but after a few moments struggle I managed to get the flap open and throw it out. It seemed like hours before we regained the cover of the ridge but all of this must have happened within the space of eight to ten minutes. ... I got my gun going again, and, thirsting for revenge, I returned to the attack. They must have thought I was finished because I caught the guns limbering up to move to another position, and revenge was sweet.

Revenge may have been sweet but the advance had been brought to its knees by the German gunners on Telegraph Hill, the ripple effect of which impacted on 6/DLI, who were ordered not to advance beyond Beaurains. Recovering from the initial shock, the German gunners began to pour an

Telegraph Hill today.

accurate and almost continuous fire on the advancing British tanks, which undoubtedly saved the day, along with the increasing number of air attacks. To make matters worse, the 5th Panzer Division was putting in an appearance across Telegraph Hill, having swung southwest from the Arras-Cambrai road.

Understandably, Miller, who was in complete ignorance of the events on Telegraph Hill, was by now a little uneasy with the general situation around him, particularly as enemy machine gun posts were still apparent in the woods between Achicourt and Agny and there were reports of enemy tanks – the advance units of the 5th Panzer Division – approaching Beaurains. With a heavy heart he gave the order to withdraw to Achicourt:

> *It became evident from this, and reports of encircling movements by the enemy, that it would be impossible to continue to hold Beaurains, and at 8.15pm I decided to withdraw to Achicourt. A Company took up a position covering the railway, B Company was already in position covering the railway east of Agny and C and D Companies were ordered to withdraw from Beaurains to Achicourt through 4/Northumberland Fusiliers, who were already holding a position on the road St Martin-Arras.*

It was at the crossroads east of Achicourt that the withdrawing Durhams and a few tanks from 4/RTR bumped into the 5th Panzer Division in the darkness. 'It was dark with the moon just rising,' wrote Peter Vaux:

> *Then we heard tanks close by, coming towards us. We hoped they were Matildas belonging to the 7th and Cacroft walked forward to talk to them. He waved his maps at the driver's visor of the first*

tank, but to his astonishment some close cropped heads popped out and he realized they were Germans. Only twelve yards seperated us from the Germans and the most attractive tracer was already sailing over our heads. (It hit Armit's tank!) Just behind, our own tanks were returning fire with enthusiasm. Cacroft beats all records in his dash back to us and then we moved back to join the others.

Chaos ensued for some minutes before both sides extricated themselves from the confusion, the survivors of the left hand column eventually finding their way back to Vimy Ridge. During this exchange Y Company of the Northumberland Fusiliers, under the command of 29-year-old Major Kenneth Clark, came into action. Positioned around the road junction where the tree lined D919 intersected the Achicourt-Beaurains road, the Fusiliers were soon subjected to a heavy tank and artillery attack from units of the 5th Panzer Division. Caught almost unawares, Kenneth Clark had little option but to stand and fight:

I deployed two platoons forward, 4 on the right and 5 on the left, and withdrew 6 into reserve some distance behind. A section of scout cars was allotted to each forward platoon. The Germans appeared to be active, not only ahead but on both flanks ... The leading tanks advanced up a sunken road and could not at first deploy out into the open ground, or at any rate they hesitated to do so. I had already got my mechanics to explore the possibilities of an abandoned anti-tank gun nearby, and with only two remaining rounds of ammunition, seized my opportunity and opened fire on the leading tank. I secured a direct hit and successfully blocked the sunken road.

But as darkness fell the enemy attack was renewed, this time supported by flamethrowers. During this attack Lieutenant Thomas Bland, commanding the Scout Car Platoon, was badly wounded, along with Corporal Winder, who continued to command his section despite the wounds to both legs. Late in the evening, with his meagre force surrounded and taking heavy casualties, Clark realized that an organized withdrawal was impossible and gave orders for the survivors to withdraw in small groups. Although a few individuals escaped from 6 Platoon, the bulk of 4 and 5 Platoons and the Scout Platoon were either killed or captured. Clark – by now wounded in the arm – was taken prisoner, along with two other officers and 166 other ranks were recorded as killed, wounded or missing; losses which accounted for over half the battalion's fighting men.

The Right Column

The column left Petit Vimy without their Northumberland Fusiliers motorcycle reconnaissance or the artillery of 365/Battery, which had been held up on the gridlocked roads to the north. Lieutenant Colonel Tim Beart, a regular soldier who had arrived in France with the 2/DLI in September 1939 and been awarded the MC in 1919, was still issuing his orders while the 8/DLI was on the move when the battalion came under fire near Maroeuil from German gunners who were ranged on the village. Ian English, one of only twenty-four officers to be awarded three MCs in the Second World War, tells us that while the column was delayed at Maroeuil the tanks of 7/RTR soon disappeared off in the distance:

> *That was the last the rest of the column saw of them. Contact was lost with the officer commanding the tanks and his liaison officer with the battalion was unable to get in touch with him at any period during the battle.*

As the infantry crossed the Arras-St Pol road (N39) the burnt out wreckage of a column of German 5.9-inch howitzers from the 8th Panzer Division were scattered around the road and dead enemy soldiers lay in

The 12/Lancers were equipped with the CS9 Armoured Car.

65

The Entrance to Duisans British Cemetery, which still bears the marks of the engagement on 21 May 1940.

confused heaps, having fallen prey to the 12/Lancers and tanks from 3 DLM. It was now quite clear that the Germans were much further north than first envisaged and were definitely between Vimy and the proposed start line. C Company was soon in action around Duisans CWGC Cemetery on the D339, to the west of Duisans. Lieutenant John Leybourne recalled that his company commander, Captain James Walton, reached the steps of the cemetery to find a German soldier peeping round one of the headstones:

Captain Walton was only armed with a pencil in one hand and a map in the other. After, what he termed, a game of hide and seek in and around the tomb stones, 20-30 prisoners were taken and a large number of dead and wounded were found as a result of the French attack. It is estimated that the cemetery had been defended by about 100-120 men, some of whom must have been part of the motorized column which had been caught earlier in the day, because there were a number of vehicles taken with machine guns mounted on motor-cycle sidecars. These machine guns were actually sited on the west and south side of the cemetery and it appears they were not ready for the attack from whence it came.

66

Corporal George Self remembered that they were fired on from the cemetery and, with the assistance of three French tanks, led by a French officer on foot, cleared the cemetery:

This Frenchman came down the road with these three tanks, walking in front of them, and then he turned into the field and led the tanks against the cemetery ... He cleared them out and some of our lads followed behind ... one of our boys was shot in the back by one of these Germans who was supposed to be dead. I suppose they [the Durhams] *lost their heads and if there was anyone else alive apart from this German they weren't alive very long.*

Some of the crews from the burnt-out vehicles had also made for the woods around Duisans Château, but were soon rooted out by B Company. Lieutenant Leybourne recalled his platoon's advance:

I called the section commanders forward and told them that the enemy had been seen in the long grass, numbers unknown, and that we would advance two sections up and one in reserve; platoon HQ in the centre. The whole operation was rushed and underway, certainly within five minutes. As we fixed bayonets I remember thinking this was really true, because I never thought it possible that I would ever have to give the order to fix bayonets ... I ran into a German soldier lying in the grass with the muzzle of his rifle pointing at me. Fortunately he stood up and put his hands up, and at the same time about a dozen others did the same thing at intervals spread over my platoon front.

Having detailed two men to escort the prisoners to the château, Leybourne and his men proceeded into Duisans, where they took up defensive positions along with C Company around the village. Second Lieutenant Ian English remembered meeting another French tank in the village, whose commander was extremely worried about the open flank. This prompted Tim Beart to order a troop of 65/Anti Tank Regiment to take up position on the western flank and approach to Duisans. This may well have been the troop that was positioned at the cemetery and who would later come under fire from French tanks who were responsible for the attack on the gunners and some of B Company at around 10.00 that evening. During this short engagement several tanks were disabled and one anti-tank gun was hit, two of the crew being wounded, before the mistake was realized. According to Lieutenant Leybourne, the French tanks could not be identified in the darkness.

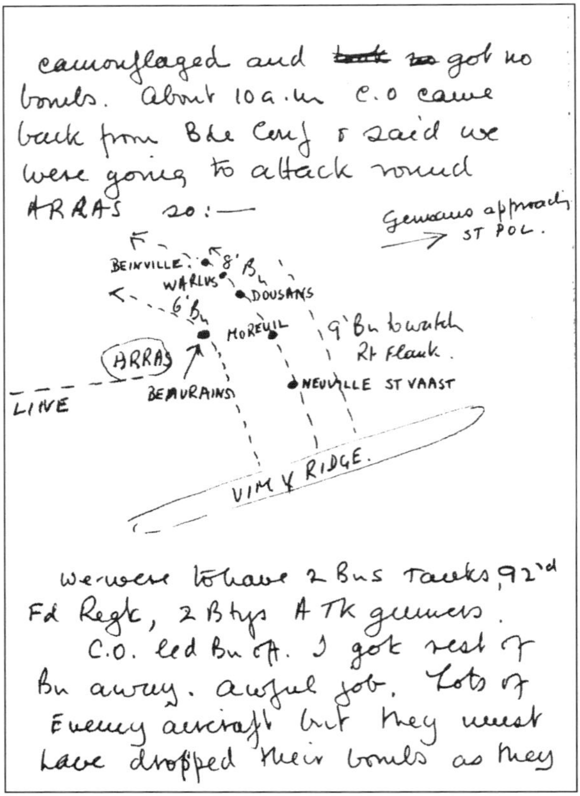

camouflaged and ~~took so~~ got no
bombs. About 10 a.m C.O came
back from Bde Conf & said we
were going to attack round
ARRAS so:—

Germans approaching
→ ST POL.

BERNVILLE 8'B
WARLUS DOUSANS
6'B
MOREUIL 9'Bn b watch
Rt Flank.
ARRAS NEUVILLE ST VAAST
BEAURAINS
LINE

VIMY RIDGE.

A page from the
diary of Major
Ross McLaren
with a hurried
sketch of the
British advance
from Vimy
Ridge.

We were to have 2 Bns Tanks 92nd
Fd Regt, 2 Btys A Tk gunners.
C.O. led Bn off. I got rest of
Bn away. awful job. Lots of
Enemy aircraft but they must
have dropped their bombs as they

Shortly after his arrival at Duisans, Lieutenant Colonel Beart decided to continue the advance with part of HQ Company, A and D Companies and the Carrier Platoon, leaving Major Ross McLaren to hold the village with B and C Companies. Lieutenant Leybourne later recalled being in the cellar of the château, where Padre Duggan was giving water to the German wounded and the Regimental Medical Officer (RMO), Lieutenant Wilkinson, was attending to wounds. 'Major McLaren poured over a map by the light of one single torch, which appeared to be the only available in the battalion.' It is likely the map was also one of the few available, although we can assume Tim Beart took another with him as he continued south.

7/RTR lose direction
Meanwhile, pressing on ahead of the infantry, 7/RTR appeared to lose direction and moved southeast towards Wailly, apparently not realizing that Warlus was one of the objectives. Had they kept to the agreed route they would certainly have found the 25th Panzer Regiment between

Commanding the 25th Panzer Regiment was *Oberst* Karl Rothenburg (second from left), who is seen sitting with Rommel and his staff. It is likely their attention is being held by aircraft of the *Luftwaffe*.

Warlus and Wanquentin on its way north to Acq and, although the German regiment possessed more tanks, they would have been hard pressed against the thicker armour of the 7/RTR Matilda IIs. As it was, the German panzers continued almost unopposed; but it is hard to believe that the level of dust thrown up by the panzers went entirely unnoticed by 7/RTR. Unfortunately for the Northumberland Fusilier's 12 Platoon, they did find the panzers between Warlus and Wanquetin and in the ensuing skirmish lost practically all their number.

7/RTR, having lost direction, now found themselves entwined with the rear units of 4/RTR, which only served to underline how far off course they had strayed. Despite none of the radio sets working Lieutenant Colonel Heyworth managed to get the regiment back on course, although, sadly, both he and the Adjutant, 31-year-old Captain Herman Kauter, were killed in the process as they attempted to redirect the confused tank commanders. Spreading out in fan formation from Dainville, 7/RTR were without their commanding

Captain Herman Kauter was Adjutant of 4/RTR.

69

Panzer 38(t) tanks of the 7ᵗʰ Panzer Division.

officer and, it appears, without their system of command. B Company now headed down the Doullens road before turning towards Wailly at le Bac du Nord, D Company trundled towards Ficheux and A Company – such as it was – moved towards Mercatel.

The French 3rd Light Mechanized Division

The advance by this column was wrapped in confusion. It had been agreed that the French tanks would screen the British right flank but they appear to have been 'kept out of the loop' as regards the time and direction of the British attack, which may account for the near fatal collision between French tanks and 260/Battery at Duisans. However, the sixty French Soma S35 tanks did provide valuable support for the beleaguered 8/DLI at Warlus and were involved in a bitter engagement with the 25th Panzer Regiment around Haute-Avenses and Agnez-lès-Duisans, presenting its commander, *Oberst* Karl Rothenburg, with some heavy casualties and a few worrying moments. They also engaged units of the SS-*Totenkopf* Division near Simecourt.

A and D Companies, 8/Durham Light Infantry

The column was now split and the DLI were completely without reliable information as to the dispositions of German forces, let alone their own. Accordingly, Colonel Beart with A and D Companies, accompanied by the Carrier Platoon, marched on towards Warlus leaving Ross McLaren in command of B and C Companies at Duisans. Second Lieutenant English recalled their approach to Warlus, when they saw a small party of Germans running into the village from the east side heading towards the church. There was no fire from this group when the scout troop had gone through the village some moments earlier, but English writes that some prisoners were taken before the battalion moved through Warlus. Advancing through the village, Captain John Dixon and A Company cleared the southern side of the village and moved past the water tower on the Rue de Berneville towards the outskirts of Berneville, which was cleared by 6.00pm. From Berneville the road rises gently towards the Arras-Doullens road, and here the advance sections ran into a heavy barrage of fire from enemy units on the road. The company was pinned down and Dixon was wounded in the head, the advance stalling under the weight of fire. The Baron von Münchhausen was a company commander with the 1st Battalion, 7th Rifle Regiment (1/IR.7), and was in the area of the crossroads on the Arras-Doullens road when he was summoned by the battalion commander:

He told me that there were still isolated nests of resistance in Berneville and I was to attack it with my company and clear it ... I deployed the company in the low ground and positioned my heavy machine guns in order to give us fire cover during the attack. We then pushed forward ... I formed all sections in extended line and told them to run as hard as they could towards the village shouting and yelling ... as we came up the slope we saw one of two people running rapidly into the village. In fact from some of the houses we were met by fire and the fire then stopped.

This final flourish by the German infantry was enough to carry them through the village and establish themselves on the far side. The Durham's advance was over and Lieutenant Colonel Beart was now at a disadvantage.

Back at Warlus, B Company and the remaining Durhams, which by this time had moved up to the water tower, came under air attack from Stuka 87bs. Their position offered little in the way of cover, a factor that was very much to the *Luftwaffe's* benefit. When faced with an enemy occupation of a village, Rommel always brought in his airborne artillery in the shape of Stuka 87bs. Warlus was no exception and Second Lieutenant English recalled the arrival of the German dive bombers:

The Junkers Ju 87 or Stuka (from *Sturzkampfflugzeug*) was used extensively as airborne artillery by German ground troops.

Well for the next twenty minutes or so there was the whine of these aircraft. They put a whistle on them which made them shriek as they came down and the crash of the bombs and strafing from machine guns made it most unpleasant. In fact, strange as it may seem now, I was more in the shape of a pancake, pressing myself into the earth. During this attack there was an ack ack [anti-aircraft] platoon truck nearby and it had a Bren gun on a tripod fixed to the truck at the back. This one gunner was firing at the planes until one of the Brigade Anti-Tank vehicles, which was 20 yards behind him, was hit and the gunner stopped firing. They knocked out that truck and two more, and afterwards we reckoned they wounded ten men, and that is all the physical and material damage they did. But the damage to morale they did was terrific, bearing in mind this was the first time we had been in action and the first time we had been directly dive bombed.

Soon after the air attack about eighteen tanks approached from the direction of Simecourt. Ian English thinks Major John Raine may have been one of the first to spot the enemy tanks:

We had at that time with us three French tanks, one of them towing another and the crews of these tanks were lying under one of the tanks. They had got there when the bombing was on and they were still there. [John Raine] saw these chaps and routed them out with his stick from under the tank. His French wasn't terribly good but he made the chap understand and he came out and fired at the leading tank, which was about fifty yards away. I don't know whether he damaged it or not, anyway the tank sheared off so that saved the situation.

Apart from the casualties, one of whom was Captain Goodenough, the German shelling set fire to haystacks and several buildings. With the situation looking precarious, Lieutenant Colonel Beart ordered A Company back to the water tower area, where they took up positions on the right flank. Two platoons from D Company were deployed on the edge of the small wood to the left of the water tower, while another was positioned in the village to cover the roads from the north. Ian English

The *Panzerkampfwagen* II, or Panzer II as it was known, was the most numerous tank in the German Panzer divisions during the invasion of France.

remembered there was a lot of enemy shelling and mortar fire going on at this time:

> *One of these shells wounded the CO; he always went round with a stick and pointed to people.* [His wounds] *just meant that he went round leaning on his stick a bit more than he did before; but we got the impression that he thought the whole thing was a bit of an exercise.*

Another difficulty that had become apparent was the lack of communication with Duisans. The Battalion wireless truck had been left behind at the château and several attempts to get a message through using dispatch riders ended in failure. Finally Beart sent Lieutenant Redvers Potts on a motor cycle, who rode the gauntlet through the German lines to report to McLaren and eventually to Brigade Headquarters at Maroeuil.

With the onset of darkness Beart withdrew the remaining Durhams into a closer perimeter. Enemy activity was heard all around them, but there was no concerted attack, apart from a few patrols that were kept at bay by rifle and Bren gun fire. But it was becoming more and more obvious that they were surrounded on all sides and it was just a matter of time before the end came.

B and C Companies, 8/Durham Light Infantry

In the meantime all attempts at contact with A and D Companies from Duisans had failed, as had attempts to get in touch with Brigade HQ at Maroeuil. McLaren rightly considered that he was surrounded and was now faced with one of the difficult decisions of command: Should he stay put as Beart had ordered or should he get out and face the possible consequences. Fortunately, Padre Duggan managed to get through to Maroeuil in a truck just before Second Lieutenant Potts arrived, *en-route* to Maroeuil. Returning to Duisans with Brigadier Churchill's orders, Potts handed over Churchill's instructions to McLaren, which simply read: 'Get out if you can'. With the 7th Panzer Division now on the Duisans-Warlus road, it was assumed Beart and his men were either killed or captured and McLaren concentrated on getting his own force away. Gathering the fit troops from around Duisans, McLaren set off across country and marched back to Maroeuil, arriving at 3.15am on 22 May

A and D Companies, 8/Durham Light Infantry

At Warlus Beart's men felt like the end was close. With ammunition running low and the noise of German reinforcements apparent all around them, they prepared themselves for the inevitable. Then, at midnight six French tanks and two APCs smashed their way through a very surprised German cordon around the village and 'rumbled into the village'. Ian English thought it was a miracle. The only way out was to run the gauntlet of German fire with the French tanks giving covering fire – which is exactly what they did. With surprise on their side and the darkness cloaking their movement, the remaining Durhams crowded into the serviceable carriers and broke out to head north towards Duisans:

Second Lieutenant Ian English.

We got everyone onto the trucks and there was nobody marching, some of the French tanks went in the front and some at the back. Before we kicked off, we patrolled down through some of the side roads in the village to see if they were clear, and they were. It was three o'clock in the morning when we left. We saw some Germans on the road between Duisans and Warlus, but they didn't interfere with us.

Arriving at Duisans, which was abandoned, they found the Battalion RMO was still at the château, and loaded him and the wounded onto the transport. The remnants of the two companies arrived back at Maroeuil sometime after dawn. McLaren later wrote in his diary that Tim Beart was sent off to hospital with a flesh wound in the thigh and he took over command of the battalion, adding that Walter Goodenough, John Dixon and Second Lieutenant Dees were all missing.

7/RTR

But what of 7/RTR, who had lost their CO and were now dispersed in and around Wailly, Mercatel and Ficheux? Earlier in the day Lieutenant Tom Craig in his Matilda II crossed the railway line a little to the south of the level crossing that had caused 4/RTR so much trouble. He was ordered to move on to Wailly after a brief halt at Achicourt:

I was entirely on my own as the other troops had not caught up. About 500 yards from [Wailly] *I was fired on by a large armoured car with a small gun on it; 20mm I suppose, with no effect on my tank. I fired back and the car burst into flames. One of the crew must have had guts as, although wounded, he continued to fire as I closed in and eventually I saw him climb out and fall in the gutter, badly burned. I moved past the blazing armoured car nearly up to the crossroads in the village, which was full of German infantry.*

Craig had arrived in Wailly at the same time at *Oberst* Georg von Bismark's 7th Rifle Regiment and, had he but known when he burst into the village, was only 1,000 yards from Rommel and his ADC *OberLeutnant* Most. But he and his crew were too preoccupied with firing on the disorganized German units to worry about anything else.

It is very clear that had Rommel not been on hand to personally direct the German response, the evident panic may well have become a rout. Having ordered the return of the 25th Panzer Regiment to join the battle, he established himself on the high point west of Wailly. At this juncture he must have realized the battle was at

Rommel was largely responsible for halting the 7/RTR advance from his vantage point on Hill 111 at le Belloy Farm.

its critical point, a knocked out Panzer III was evidence enough that tanks from D Company 7/RTR had already crossed the minor Wailly-Berneville road and some of B Company's tanks were moving up from the Doullens road, sending German gunners running for their lives. Dealing first with the attack from the north, before turning his attention to the threat from the west, Rommel turned every available gun onto the oncoming tanks. His diary provides us with a glimpse of the extraordinary energy he displayed in dealing with the threat from British tanks:

Half a mile east of [Wailly] *we came under fire from the north. One of our howitzer batteries was already in position at the northern exit of the village, firing rapidly on enemy tanks attacking southwards from Arras ... Most and I ran on ahead of the armoured cars towards the battery position. It did not look as though the battery would have much difficulty in dealing with the enemy tanks, for the gunners were calmly hurling round after round into them in complete disregard of the return fire ... We drove off to a hill, west of the village. Here we found a light anti-aircraft troop and several anti-tank guns located in some hollows in a small wood ...With Most's help, I brought every available gun into action at top speed against the tanks. Every gun, both ack ack and anti-tank was ordered to open rapid fire immediately and I*

76

personally gave each gun its target. With the enemy tanks so close, only rapid fire from every gun could save the situation. We ran from gun to gun. The objections that the range was too great, made by the gun commanders, was overruled. All I cared about was to halt the enemy tanks by heavy gunfire.

Rommel was on Hill 111 near le Belloy Farm and it was from here that he directed the battle, bringing the 7/RTR advance to a halt with the guns of the 59th and 86th Light Anti-Aircraft Batteries and elements of the 42nd Anti-Tank Battalion. It was a repeat performance of the 105mm guns on Telegraph Hill that had been the demise of 4/RTR. However, at Wailly it was not the heavy calibre guns that did the real damage, unbelievably many of the British tanks were destroyed after kit, lashed to the outside, caught fire. The British attack may have been stopped but Rommel's divisional report provides an insight into the chaos and confusion the attack caused:

While the 25th Panzer is making its attack [on the 8/DLI at Warlus], *the main body of the division is subjected to a surprise attack by a strong force of tanks followed by infantry down the line at Dainville ... Heavy fighting continued between 15.30 and 19.00hours against hundreds* [sic] *of the enemy's tanks ... our own anti-tank guns were not powerful enough, even at short range, to defeat the English tanks. The defensive front built by the anti-tank guns were broken through by the enemy, the guns destroyed or over-run, the crews mostly killed. Finally it was possible to hold this heavy attack by the defensive fire of all batteries ... and after the loss of many tanks the enemy drew back to Arras.*

Rommel had managed to bring the tank advance to a halt by firmly demonstrating the importance of forward command but, as the death of *OberLeutnant* Most – who was standing by his side – underlined, it was a style of command that carried its risks.

The attack by King and Doyle
There was one audacious attack by two Matilda IIs from A Company 7/RTR carried out by Major John King and Sergeant Ben Doyle. Whilst this may have highlighted the bravery of these two tank commanders, it also drew sharp attention to the vulnerability of tanks without the close support of artillery and infantry. It was near Mercatel where it is thought the first recorded instance of the 88mm gun was used against British tanks and within months the gun was to achieve an almost legendary status

The 88mm flak gun was a dual purpose weapon that was used as both an anti-aircraft and anti-tank gun. This particular gun was captured in Normandy in 1944 and is fitted with an armoured shield to protect the gunners, denoting it was used in an anti-tank-role.

amongst tank crews. However, apart from its range and effectiveness, the use of the 88mm gun should not have been a surprise to the Allies, for it had been used frequently in the Spanish Civil War in both the anti-tank and anti-aircraft role and German blitzkrieg doctrine saw the armoured spearheads moving with their own anti-aircraft guns for protection, including the 88mm.

Having begun the day with seven Matilda IIs, the two remaining tanks of King's company careered through German held territory shooting at everything that moved and no doubt causing innumerable German gunners considerable anxiety as their anti-tank rounds failed to penetrate the British armour. King recalled running over several guns:

> *Suddenly we came under fire of 3 or 4 guns about 300 yards to our front. They did not penetrate, so we went straight at them, and put them out of action. My tank ran over one, and I saw another suffer the same fate. Small parties of enemy machine gunners and infantry now kept getting up in front of us, and retreating rapidly, giving us good MG targets for about 10 minutes.*

Further on they came across four enemy tanks and a roadblock. King wrote that the tanks were about the same size as his Matilta II and were armed with a turret mounted gun and a machine gun. These tanks may well have been Panzer IIIs:

> They were firing at the Matilda 1s and when they saw me the two rear tanks swung their guns round in my direction. We opened fire together, and I advanced up the road, Sgt Doyle following, but unfortunately with his fire masked by my tank. Their shells did not penetrate ... my 2-pounders went right through them. By the time I reached them, two were in flames and some men from one of the others were running over the fields. I passed between them and went hard at the weakest part of the roadblock.

Isolated but still moving, King called up Doyle and, reassured to find he was still intact, they both pressed on, by now fully aware they were outnumbered and had a slim chance of survival. Doyle recounts the events of the next hour:

A photograph, that is said to depict the two A Company tanks commanded by King and Doyle, under fire from a German 88mm gun, which looks as though it has hurriedly been adapted for use as an anti-tank weapon.

Then the fun started. I know at least five German tanks he put out of action and a number of trucks etc. You see we met a convoy, and we did have some fun. We paid the jerry back for the loss of the rest of the company, and about 8.00pm, I saw him get hit in the front locker, but he still kept going. I myself was then on fire, but he must have been on fire for an hour or so. He would not leave his tank because we were surrounded by German tanks, so we just kept on, letting them have it.

Despite their tanks being finally hit and rendered unserviceable, both crews survived and for a short time evaded capture until they were rounded up.

Casualties

The British had paid a very heavy price for their defeat and, as is often the case, exact casualty numbers are imprecise. The CWGC data base records twenty-three identified casualties from the two Durham Light Infantry battalions, of which five are commemorated on the Dunkirk Memorial, along with seventeen from the two tank regiments, who were killed in action on 21 May. The RNF have six identified deaths from Y and Z Companies between the 21-22 May. Ian English maintains that 6/DLI suffered over 200 casualties and 8/DLI had over 100 killed, wounded or missing, largely from A and D Companies. What these figures do not tell us is the number of wounded who escaped capture or how many later died of their wounds, like the unfortunate Lieutenant Bland of the 4/RNF on 30 May.

The official history of the 7th Panzer Division states that their losses on 21 May were eighty-nine killed, 116 wounded and 173 missing. Rommel probably lost some forty tanks and, according to German sources, forty-seven British tanks were disabled, twenty-eight of them being destroyed by the guns of AR 78. A glance at Rommel's battle maps show quite clearly his artillery units deployed with the advanced formations, supporting Rommel's claim that his deployment of artillery was a decisive factor on the battle. We have little choice but to view losses on this scale, without any gain in ground, as a crippling defeat for the British and it is fortunate that the Germans were under the misapprehension that the attack was part of a larger coordinated strategic counter attack against them. There is no precise data concerning French losses, but 3/DLM probably lost in excess of twenty tanks.

Civilian Massacres

What is often ignored are the civilian atrocities committed by the *SS-*

Totenkopf Division as they advanced north, reflecting what can only be described as revenge. Certainly the timing and extent of the killings coincided with the losses experienced by the battalion during the British counterstroke of 21 May as the division searched outlying villages and hamlets for evading British soldiers. We have already mentioned Mercatel, where eight *SS* Gunners were killed during the British advance; here six civilians were shot without apparent reason, including, it is said, three Belgian refugees who were seeking shelter in the village. But this was only the beginning. At Habarcq several civilians were shot, including a father and his seventeen year old son, while at Aubigny-en-Artois, sixty-four civilian hostages were executed in the local quarry on 22 May. Today a memorial stands on the site of the quarry on Rue de 22 Mai 1940 and the victims lie in the communal cemetery. Other massacres took place at two local farms bringing the total number killed at Aubigny-en-Artois to ninety-eight. At Simencourt five civilian men were killed and at Hermanville another four civilians were killed. In ten days the *SS-Totenkopf* Division shot 264 civilians and executed a further 130.

The memorial at Aubigny-en-Artois, where sixty-four civilians were executed by the *SS-Totenkopf* Division on 22 May.

81

Chapter Five

The Scarpe Valley – East

As Franklyn's plan took shape in the form of the curving sweep to the south and east of Arras, it was intended that the 13 Brigade battalions, who were positioned along the Scarpe to the east of Arras, would cross the river with the object of extending the gains made on 21 May as far as the River Sensée. The plan, which was received with some enthusiasm at Gort's Headquarters, struck Franklyn as 'a case of the tail wagging the dog'. This sector of the Scarpe valley was held initially by two battalions from 69 Brigade (Brigadier John Downe), 23rd Division, until the early hours of 21 May, and then by four battalions from 150 and 13 Brigades; their river frontage facing the heights of Monchy-le Preux and Boiry-Notre-Dame. The infantry units deployed along the Scarpe were as follows:

The Scarpe at Fampoux was an effective anti-tank barrier.

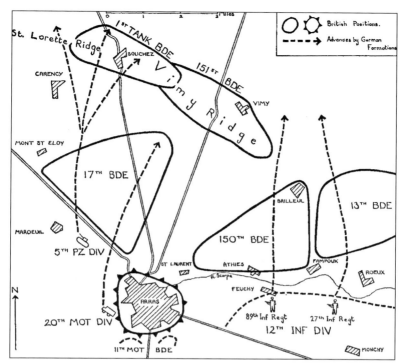

A map taken from *The Shadow of Vimy Ridge* depicting the British and German deployments east and west of Arras along the Scarpe Valley.

6th Battalion Yorkshire Regiment (Green Howards)

Badly equipped and only partially trained, this 23rd Division battalion spent the first half of May working on the aerodrome near Grévilliers. Commanded by Lieutenant Colonel Steel, the battalion arrived on the north bank of the Scarpe at dawn on 20 May. B, C and D Companies were deployed along the river, with A and HQ Companies in reserve. Two companies of 11/Durham Light infantry were on the battalion's left flank with the 5/East Yorkshires at Plouvain. Apart from German mortar fire on the forward positions, no attempt was made by the Germans to cross the river. In the early hours of 21 May the battalion was relieved by 4/Green Howards from the 50th Division.

5th Battalion East Yorkshire Regiment

This territorial Yorkshire battalion was another 23rd Division battalion largely employed on airfield construction duties near Grévilliers and was, again, only partly equipped and trained. Under the command of Lieutenant Colonel D J Keating, the battalion arrived at Plouvain at 6.30am on 20 May. Within two hours German mortars on the opposite bank had caused fourteen casualties in B Company. French sappers blew the bridges in the neighbourhood at 9.00am. Relieved on 21 May, the battalion moved back to Thélus after a very short period in the front line.

4th Battalion Yorkshire Regiment (Green Howards)
This 50th Division battalion was deployed to Athies on 20 May. Lieutenant Colonel Charles Littleboy gave orders for the battalion to move to the crossroads north of Athies and, along with his Intelligence Officer, Lieutenant Peter Kirby, and the Anti-Tank Platoon Commander, Second Lieutenant Roche, arrived in Athies at midnight. Liaising with the 6/Green Howards at Roeux, Littleboy expressed some surprise at discovering Steel's men had been given orders to withdraw. Littleboy positioned his men along the two mile front with B Company (Captain Ian Donkin) holding the railway bridge area, D Company (Major H Keyworth) positioned to hold Athies and the road bridge over the Scarpe and C Company (Captain Ben Proud) on the left flank, in the outskirts of Fampoux. A Company (Captain Bob Metcalf), the mortar platoon and some of HQ Company, were kept in reserve. Battalion HQ was established at an estaminet at the crossroads in Athies. The carrier platoon was hidden in a sunken road northwest of Fampoux.

2nd Battalion Wiltshire Regiment
Commanded by Lieutenant Colonel Eric Moore, the battalion arrived at Fampoux at around 6.00am on 21 May and deployed along a 4,000 yard frontage between Fampoux and the quarry east of Roeux. On the right flank, Moor deployed D Company (Captain Charles Bond) with B Company (Captain C F Read) holding the Roeux Bridge area. On the left flank was C Company (Captain Lord Arundell), with A Company (Captain James Heulin) in the gap between B and D Companies.

Lieutenant Colonel E▶ Moore commanded tʰ 2/Wiltshires.

2nd Battalion Royal Inniskilling Fusiliers
The battalion arrived on the Scarpe at 6.00am on 21 May and occupied a long front of some 2,000 yards running from Plouvain to Biache-St-Vaast. Lieutenant Colonel Frederick Lefroy deployed A Company in Biache-St-Vaast, B Company to hold the centre ground and C Company, together with HQ Company, in Plouvain. D Company was held in reserve, immediately behind the C Company positions. Battalion HQ was in a 'brick field by the railway embankment' north of Plouvain. One platoon of A Company was ordered to hold the bridge at Biache-St-Vaast.

Carriers of the 2/Royal Inniskillings at St-Aubin earlier in 1940.

The lock gates and road bridge at Biache-St-Vaast were held by A Company, 2/Royal Inniskillings.

2nd Battalion Cameronians (Scottish Rifles)

The battalion was under the command of Major Cyril Barclay, as Lieutenant Colonel George 'Pop' Gilmore was still trying to reach the battalion after returning from leave. The battalion arrived at Fresnes-les-Montauban at 6.00am on 21 May and, apart from one company that was detached to guard Brigade HQ at Gavrelle, the battalion went into Brigade reserve north of Roeux. At 1.00pm D Company (Captain Robert Miller), having marched from Gavrelle, was ordered forward to hold the bridge area at Roeux and defend 252/Field Company, who were constructing a pontoon bridge. Robert Miller was killed while the company was at Gavrelle and his place was taken by Captain T A Hickman. The original bridge had been blown but not sufficiently to prevent enemy infantry from crossing. Two platoons were positioned to hold the ground on either side of the road and a small patrol was despatched across the river to gather intelligence. A Company (Captain Sir Edward Bradford) was divided into three groups and detailed to advance across the bridge and move towards Pelves, Monchy-le-Preux and Boiry-Notre-Dame.

20-24 May

The three battalions of 150 Brigade were just to the south of Dottignies when they were relieved on 19 May by the 1st Division and were added to the growing number of units that made up Frankforce. Arriving at Farbus, the commanding officer of the 4/Green Howards was summoned to Vimy, where he was told that the 5/Green Howards has been sent to join the Arras garrison, the 4/East Yorkshires were moving to St-Laurent-Blangy and he was to deploy his battalion at Athies, to hold the bridges over the Scarpe. An old soldier himself, Lieutenant Colonel Littleboy had lost an older brother – Lieutenant Wilfred Littleboy – in the First World War and was acutely aware that the battalion had fought in the Second Battle of the Scarpe in 1917, just a few miles from Athies. By 10.30am on 21 May, Littleboy was sufficiently satisfied with his defence to allow the French outposts to withdraw.

The 2/Wiltshires were near Seclin on 19 May when orders reached Lieutenant Colonel Moore to move south through Lens to take up bridge guard duties between Lens and Harnes. *En-route* these orders were changed again, Captain George Woolnough, the battalion Adjutant, remembered being quite flabbergasted at the frequent change in orders that finally sent the battalion to take over the bridgeheads at Fampoux and Roeux on the Scarpe:

At 1.30am [on 21 May] *we set off by march route directly south from Mericourt through Bailleul arriving at Fampoux about*

6.00am ... Just before we arrived at Fampoux the CO
[commanding officer] *and the Reconnaissance Group went ahead
and were followed half an hour later by* [the company
commanders]. *When the CO got to Roeux to take over, he found
the 6th Battalion, The Green Howards were already in positions
on the river line. He had to make a very quick decision, because
the battalion was coming up close behind and he gave out his
orders to his company commanders for taking over this position.
The Green Howards marched out at 7.00am.*

Lieutenant Colonel Moore was faced with a wide frontage along the
banks of the Scarpe. The 6/Green Howards had deployed all four rifle
companies along the river and, with time at a premium, Moore felt he
had little choice but to take over these positions by placing all four of his
companies along the river, keeping his Carrier Platoon as a mobile
reserve. Battalion Headquarters was, in the words of Captain Woolnough,
'half way between the level crossing and the Roeux Bridge in a large
house on the east of the road'. The building was shared with the battalion
aid post and the two Forward Observation Officers from 9 and 91/Field
Regiments. However, it was quite obvious to all concerned that the whole
position was in direct view of German observers on the south bank, as
was every vehicle travelling along the road leading north to Gavrelle.
 In May 1940 the village of Roeux, as were the other villages along the
Scarpe, much smaller than today. The river featured a number of large
woods on both sides, the remnants of which can still be seen. When the
Wiltshires arrived on the Scarpe both the bridges at Roeux and Fampoux
had been blown, although at Roeux the break in the bridge was on the
northern side, and it was still possible for determined infantry to cross
using planks to bridge the gap.
 The Roeux Bridge was the scene of considerable activity by 252/Field
Company, who were constructing a pontoon bridge across the Scarpe to
aid the advance in support of the 151 Brigade attack the next day. D
Company, 2/Cameronians, who were being held in Brigade reserve at
Fresnes, were ordered forward to protect the construction of the bridge
and took the opportunity to put a platoon under Second Lieutenant Kettles
across the river to capture a German despatch rider. Kettles was awarded
the MC for this exploit.
 Rather surprisingly, the events of 21 May had very little impact on
the line of the Scarpe, although three German tanks did put in an
appearance in front of the Green Howards' D Company, prompting PSM
(Platoon Sergeant Major) Upton to disable the leading vehicle with a
Boys rifle. Later that evening, Captain Ian Donkin took a small patrol

The modern day bridge at Roeux.

across the river to investigate Upton's tank, returning with a map and some papers. [Donkin was killed in May 1942 when his hospital ship was attacked by German aircraft on her way to Alexandria from Tobruk.] Nevertheless, the failure of the counterstroke around the western and southern aspects of Arras meant the pontoon bridge at Roeux was now surplus to requirements; although the events of 23 May brought the bridge once more back into the glare of publicity.

The Wiltshires' deployment on the Green Howards' left flank had enabled Lieutenant Colonel Littleboy to shorten his front on 22 May by withdrawing C Company and the Carrier Platoon from Fampoux; a task that had barely been completed when, rather unexpectedly, orders to withdraw arrived at 4.00pm. As the trucks arrived in daylight under a

Captain Ian Donkin was drowned when hi[s] hospital ship was sun[k] in May 1942.

huge cloud of dust, German shellfire followed them to the loading points where the vehicles were loaded with the battalion's baggage under more or less incessant shellfire. The regimental historian recorded the bombardment that followed:

But before any troops moved, the enemy put down a heavy barrage of mortar, shell and machine gun fire onto B and D Companies and it was reported the Germans had crossed the canal in front of B Company ... At 11.30pm the orders to withdraw were cancelled and the transport brought back once more the baggage it had evacuated earlier in the evening.

Under cover of the barrage German infantry had temporarily established themselves near the railway bridge at Fampoux during a brief engagement that cost the lives of Second Lieutenant Austin Capps and two of his men. With Athies in flames, Littleboy withdrew Battalion Headquarters to a command post further back on the ridge, leaving Lieutenant Kirby in the attic of the estaminet at the Athies crossroads to observe and report to Littleboy. It was, wrote the battalion historian, 'an unhealthy observation post, which became unhealthier when the Estaminet caught fire'. Kirby's award of the MC was well deserved. [Badly wounded in the Libyan desert, he was invalided home in 1943 and ended his war in command of the Battle Camp at Capel Curig in Wales.] Orders for the withdrawal were brought by Kendal Chavasse, the 150 Brigade Major, who it seems had an eventful drive from Brigade Headquarters. 'It was a hair raising drive,' he wrote, 'of course I could use no lights, and there was a fog.' Nevertheless, the orders got through and Littleboy extracted his battalion. Chavasse's brother-in-law, Lieutenant Perceval-Maxwell, was serving with the 6/DLI and had been taken prisoner the previous day.

Back on the Wiltshire's front it would appear that a crossing by enemy infantry was also made between B and D Companies; however, a hastily dispatched company of the Cameronians prevented any permanent lodgement and by midnight it had been confirmed by the Wiltshires D Company Commander, Captain Dick Bond, that the *status quo* had been established. [Bond was killed by a sniper in 1944 while serving with B Squadron, 1st Special Air Service Regiment, in Germany.] Preparations for an enemy assault across the river were clearly in evidence and the guns of 91/Field Regiment were constantly in action against targets on the far bank. One of these was a complete German bridging team

Captain Dick Bond was killed in 1944.

that emerged from Monchy-le Preux; needless to say, 91/Field Regiment, shooting from south of Gavrelle, denied their advance to the river, inflicting severe casualties and dispersing the enemy troops. It is not clear whether it was this incident, or the reports from a Wiltshires' patrol that crossed the river to find it clear of the enemy, which contributed to the foray across the river by B Company. The orders for the Wiltshires 'excursion' came from 44-year-old Brigadier Miles Dempsy, commanding 13 Brigade. After a party of the Wiltshires repaired the pontoon bridge at Roeux, Captain Read and B Company began to cross with, presumably, a view to establishing a bridgehead. Quite what Dempsy intended by this surprising turn of events remains unclear but the outcome was disastrous for B

Brigadier Miles Dempsy commanded 13 Brigade in 1940 and was the first British Army commander to cross the Rhine in 1945.

Company. When two platoons had crossed and moved forward, seemingly without enemy interference, heavy machine gun fire opened up from both flanks, pinning them to the ground. They had been ambushed. Communications were non-existent and it was left to Second Lieutenant Chivers to swim across the river under fire to report that withdrawal from the enemy trap was the only course open to the survivors. Only Captain Read and about thirty survivors accompanied Chivers on his third and last swim back to the Wiltshire lines. What made matters worse was that B Company's foray across the river now left a large gap in the Wiltshires' defences, which was partially filled by the Carrier Platoon and Captain Lord Arundell's C Company.

The German response was not long in coming and after a violent artillery bombardment, which began at 4.10pm, the enemy attack forced a crossing over the river and quickly infiltrated around both flanks of the battalion. The relative ease in which the German 12th Division managed to cross the river on 23 May was, in no small part, down to the withdrawal of the Cameronians to Vimy to strengthen the considerably diminished 150 Brigade. Such a drastic step underlined Franklyn's belief that Vimy Ridge was the key to the whole position, which it may well have been, but at considerable cost to the Wiltshires! The situation had now become extremely serious, a view that had not escaped those at Brigade Headquarters. At 9.30pm orders were received to withdraw to Gavrelle under the cover of darkness. But it was already too late for C Company, who were overwhelmed by units of IR27, only about half of the company getting back to Battalion Headquarters. Captain Lord Arundell was badly wounded and captured, along with Major Henry Bearne and three platoon commanders. Lord Arundell was later repatriated but died of wounds in Chester Military Hospital in September 1944.

With news that C Company was all but eliminated, Captain Woolnough recalled the dilemma now facing his commanding officer:

He realized his only two active companies left were A and D on the right and unless they were extricated at once they would be cut off and we would not have anyone left to defend [Gavrelle]. *So he gave orders for the withdrawal to begin, and this was sent off by motorcycle DR to D Company in Fampoux and the CO went off himself to Fampoux to take out A Company ... D Company, having had the message, withdrew first; as they got into the village they were fired on, they stopped and worked their way through the back streets and eventually regained the correct road to Gavrelle ... A Company were met by fire from the village and the company commander* [Captain J Heulin] *and a lot of Company HQ were wounded. The second in command of the company went forward, made a very quick appreciation of the situation, turned the company about and marched out through Roeux, north of the railway line.*

Captain Heulin and those wounded who were unable to continue were taken prisoner. Heulin continued to take every opportunity to annoy his captors and, after a stay in a number of POW camps, arrived at Colditz in September 1944.

Verbal orders to withdraw reached the Green Howards at 3.00am on 24 May, which was too late for Captain Ben Proud and C Company, who had borne the brunt of the German attack on 23 May. Proud and most of the company were taken prisoner, news that was later confirmed by Lieutenant Richard Booth, who had managed to extricate himself and a handful of men. As the remaining members of the battalion marched the eighteen miles to Carvin under the cover of a thick mist, Littleboy wrote in his diary, 'for the first time, I began to wonder whether the BEF withdrawal was not becoming a retreat'.

The German 12th Division aimed its attacks on 23/24 May at the vulnerable points between the villages. Although the men of IR89 had little problem crossing between Athies and Fampoux, IR27 struggled initially on the outskirts of Rouex before overcoming the Wiltshire opposition. The Inniskillings repulsed an early attack on their positions, but during a later attack their right flank was turned relatively easily by

IR27 advancing from Roeux. A number of B Company were killed and wounded and had to be left behind. Lieutenant Colonel Lefroy was faced with extracting his battalion under fire, an exercise which, Second Lieutenant William Megaw, a platoon commander with A Company, recalled, was treated with typical coolness by his commanding officer:

> *There he was, smacking his stick on his leg and smoking his pipe, and I'm sure there were bullets flying about. He said to me 'The Brigadier has decided to break off this little party and I want you to take your platoon and go out'... We had no maps of any sort so you watched the platoon in front of you and made jolly sure you didn't lose them.'*

It was Lefroy's bold handling of the Carrier Platoon that contributed to the battalion getting away relatively intact. But it was touch and go, as the British were also faced with the enemy emerging from the Green Howards' sector across the spur north of the railway line. Lefroy's luck would run out on the Ypres-Comines Canal where he was taken prisoner on 27 May 1940. By the time the Arras Garrison had received orders to evacuate the city, control of the D42, running along the northern bank of the Scarpe, had been lost and the two remaining battalions of the beleaguered 13 Brigade were reduced to fighting to hold the Douai road.

Casualties
The Green Howards' war diary tell us little about the number of casualties and simply reports that four officers and many other ranks were reported missing. However, we know that the battalion lost the majority of their C Company before they managed to extricate themselves. On 25 May the 2/Wiltshires war diary listed nine officers killed, wounded or missing and reported two rifle companies were composed of fifty men and another at eighty. It not unreasonable to estimate the battalion was probably operating at less than two thirds of its original strength. The Inniskillings' war diary does not mention the numbers killed and wounded and, although it is assumed their casualties were not as great as the Wiltshires, they did begin the campaign at nearly a quarter under strength. The Cameronians appear to have suffered only light casualties and these were mainly the result of enemy shellfire on 22 May. However, the war diary does mention some casualties from enemy bombing occurring in D Company.

Cemeteries
St-Laurent-Blangy Communal Cemetery is difficult to locate amongst the ever increasing development in the area. It is in a triangle of ground,

with the main entrance on Rue de 14 Julliet. After entering the cemetery turn right to find the five headstones in the southern corner. Sadly one is unidentified. All three identified casualties are from the East Yorkshire Regiment.

Athies Communal Cemetery Extension can be found on the D42, which runs east from St-Laurent-Blangy. As you approach the roundabout in Athies, the cemetery is on the left. The extension contains over 300 casualties of the First World War and forty-one Second World War burials, ten of which are unidentified. You will find the 1940 plot down some steps in a small garden between the extension and the communal cemetery. The most senior officer killed in May 1940 was 33-year-old **Captain Hon Anthony Phillimore** (2.A.17), a staff captain with GHQ, who was killed on 23 May, possibly during the evacuation of Arras or while attempting to contact one of the battalions along the Scarpe. Of the twenty three men from the 4/Green Howards buried here, sixteen were killed between 21 and 24 May, with another seven listed as being killed between 10 and 24 May. As the battalion was not deployed to the area until 20 May, we can be sure that all these men were casualties of the fighting at Athies. Here you will find **Second Lieutenant Austin Capps,**

Athies Communal Cemetery Extension.

(2.B.18) who was serving with B Company, Green Howards, when he was killed with two of his men on 22 May. It is likely his men are buried next to him, one of whom may have been **Lance Corporal John Furness** (2.B.16), whose family would have waited for some time before finally getting confirmation of his death.

Lance Corporal John Furness.

    Guardsman David Williams (2.B.1) and **John Daley** (2.A.18) were serving in the Carrier Platoon, Welsh Guards, when they were killed with Lieutenant Furness during the evacuation of Arras on 24 May. The grave of **Paul Dubois** is the only Frenchman in the plot, he was killed serving with the 11th Dragoons. While in the communal cemetery you could pay your respects at the single First World War grave of **Private S C Phillip**, RAMC, who was killed in April 1917.

Fampoux Communal Cemetery can be found on the D42 opposite the church and next to the war memorial, where there is plenty of parking. The British plot is to the right of the main entrance. Of the ten casualties buried here, only four are identified and, of these, three men are from the 4/Green Howards. **Second Lieutenant Hubert Wintersladen** was 21-years-old when he was killed on 24 May. Commissioned in February

Fampoux Communal Cemetery.

1939, this former Uppingham schoolboy was most probably killed as the battalion was withdrawing. It is more than likely that **Private Benjamin Urwin** and **Lance Corporal Harold Foster** were also killed during the battalion's move north. The single identified soldier of the Wiltshire Regiment is 31-year-old **Private Albert Angell,** who died of wounds on 29 May, presumably while he was a prisoner.

Roeux Communal Cemetery is best found by following the D42 from Fampoux across the railway line and the motorway to the level crossing. Take the first road on the left after the crossing and the communal cemetery is another 900 yards further down the Chemin de Croisette on the right. There is parking outside. There are thirty casualties of the Second World War here, of which ten are unidentified. Nine of the twelve 2/Wiltshires casualties may well have been killed during the crossing of the River Scarpe on 23 May and, of these, **Sergeant Robert Wright** may have died in captivity on 29 May. **Lance Sergeant Alfred Deacon** and **Private Albert Sandall** were both killed on 22 May. The six Cameronians who were killed on 23 May all probably received their fatal wounds by the bridge at Roeux, with **WOII Thomas Windle** succumbing to his wounds the next day.

Pelves Communal Cemetery is at the junction of Rue Transversale and Rue de l'Église on the D33E, which leads out of the village towards Monchy-le-Preux. There is an entrance on both sides of the 'triangle'. The three 2/Wiltshires casualties were part of the B Company excursion across the river on 23 May. **Privates Frederick Barnett**, **Ernest Mundy** and **John Radford** are buried together at the northern end of the cemetery. John Radford was 20-years old and last seen firing a Bren gun from the hip to allow the remainder of his section to withdraw back across the river.

John Radford.

Plouvain Communal Cemetery can be found on the D46 from Roeux, which passes the former quarry on the right where C Company, 2/Wiltshires were positioned. After crossing over the E17 the cemetery is 400 yards further along the road on the left. There is plenty of parking. Immediately on entering the cemetery you will see four graves in the left and a further two against the wall on the right. There are six casualties of the Second World War here, one of which is unidentified. 21-year-old

95

Private Cecil Hawkins and 35-year-old Lance Sergeant Walter Mitchelson, 5/East Yorkshires, both died of wounds resulting from the German mortar attack while serving with B Company at Plouvain. The Battalion historian reported another twelve men were wounded in the attack. The two Royal Inniskilling Fusiliers, Lance Sergeant Francis Quinn and Lance Corporal Robert Macmillan, may have died during the confusion that accompanied the battalion's withdrawal, which is probably the case with Private Arthur Jennings, 2/Wiltshires.

Biache-St-Vaast Communal Cemetery

The Communal Cemetery is on the northern side of the village on the D43 to Fresnes-les-Montauban. There is plenty of parking in the adjacent car park. The three British graves are to the right of the circular war memorial. Apart from the unidentified soldier from the Royal Armoured Corps, the remaining two are both RAF pilots. 23-year-old Warrant Officer Dennis Burman was flying a Spitfire IX from 74 Squadron when he was shot down near Roeux on 16 August 1944. He was seen to bail out but nothing more was heard until some weeks later, when it was learnt that he had been shot out of hand by the Germans to whom he surrendered. Flight Lieutenant Ian Soden was flying a Hurricane from 56 Squadron when he was shot down by a ME 110 on 18 May 1940.

Hamblain-les-Prés Communal Cemetery is situated on the southern outskirts of the village on the D34 to Boiry-Notre-Dame. On the southern side of the main path, near the entrance, are the graves of three casualties from the 2/Inniskilling Fusiliers. 20-year-old Second Lieutenant Hugh Kerrich was serving with B Company when he was killed leading a patrol across the river on 23 May. Second Lieutenant William Megaw remembered the patrol going across the river in some assault boats. 'They were badly shot up and the second lieutenant in charge of the patrol, called Kerrich, a friend of mine, was killed.' Fusiliers Edward Donaghy and Cecil Maitland were killed with Kerrich during the same patrol.

Gavrelle Communal Cemetery is south of the D33 on Rue du Plouvain and the seven British graves lie on each side of the main pathway from the entrance. The men buried here are from 13 Brigade, of which 23-year-old Lance Corporal Sydney Higgs, 2/Wiltshires, was probably killed during the battalion's withdrawal from the Scarpe on 23 May. Fuslier Joseph Conlan was killed on 18 May while the battalion was being held in reserve at Gavrelle. Born at Annetermore, County Tyrone, 29-year-old

Gavrelle Communal Cemetery.

Joe worked as a labourer. His comrade, **Fusilier Joseph McCutcheon**, was killed on the same day and they were both buried by Gavrelle residents (interviewed in the 1980s) that night in the village cemetery. They also state that five other British casualties were buried in the same cemetery in the following days. This accounts for the two gunners from 52/Anti Tank Regiment, **Rifleman Sam Culley** of the Cameronians and 36-year-old **Private John Mouser**, who was attached to the Cameronians from the RAOC.

Chapter Six

The Scarpe Valley – West

On the night of 21 May, Franklyn realized he would have to commit Brigadier Montague Stopford's 17 Brigade to prolong the defence of Arras along the line of the River Scarpe, west of Arras. He had received warnings from the 12/Lancers that two columns of the 5th Panzer Division were moving round his right flank; but it was not until after midday on 22 May that the leading battalion of 17 Brigade arrived to relieve the French. The six thousand yard front along the Scarpe was held on the left flank by the Royal Scots Fusiliers, who were in touch with the Seaforth Highlanders in the centre. On the right flank the Northamptons were in touch with the French at Mont-St-Eloi. It was a hastily conceived and very short lived deployment.

Brigadier Montague Stopford commanded 17 Brigade in 1940. The photo was taken in 1945.

2/Northamptons

Referred to amongst themselves as the 58th [of foot] and commanded by Lieutenant Colonel John Hinchliffe, the battalion arrived on the Scarpe at 1.00pm. A Company (Captain Robert Melsome) held the thickly wooded Bois de la Ville and B Company (Major Charles Watts) was positioned on the centre high ground, with one platoon forward at

The 2nd Battalion Northamptonshire Regiment on parade in 1935.

Maroeuil British Cemetery. D Company (Captain Derrick Houchin) held the north western segment of Maroeuil and C Company (Captain Alexander Norman) was held in reserve. Battalion HQ was in a 'wooded field' north of the Communal Cemetery at Maroeuil, together with one platoon of 17 Brigade Anti-Tank Platoon, under the command of Lieutenant Smith. Artillery support was from a French regiment of 75mm guns in position on the far side of Vimy Ridge.

Major Charles Watts.

6/Seaforth Highlanders
The battalion moved into position at around 4.30pm and occupied the centre ground between the Northamptons and Royal Scots Fusiliers. Their frontage ran from the eastern end of Maroeuil, which was held by A Company, to Anzin-St-Aubin. The battalion was commanded by Lieutenant Colonel W Reid, who established his Battalion HQ in Maroeuil, with C Company on the left flank and D Company in reserve.

2/Royal Scots Fusiliers
During the battle the commanding officer, Lieutenant Colonel 'Bill' Tod, was on leave and, together with several other officers in the battalion, had been trying to return to France since 10 May. Commanding the battalion in his absence was Major Piercy Morrison. The battalion's right flank was in touch with the Seaforth Highlanders and the left flank positioned in the outskirts of Arras, where D Company (Captain John Vaughn) held the area around the Ste-Catherine bridge.

Major Piercy Morrison was commanding the Royal Scots in the absence of Lieutenant Colonel Todd.

22-23 May
Captain Derrick Houchin remembered the battalion arrived on the Scarpe at 1.00pm on 22 May after being attacked by the *Luftwaffe*. Preceding the battalion, the commanding officer found a group of French officers and men in Maroeuil, who stated the Germans were close at hand and were advancing along the road on which they were about to retire. Lieutenant Colonel Hinchliffe's suggestion that they remain where they were appeared not to be the answer they had been looking for and they soon departed. In the event the 'advancing Germans' turned out to a

The River Scarpe at Maroeuil.

column of 12/Lancers! However, soon after the battalion had got into position, the enemy *were* seen on the forward slope of the ground on the opposite side of the Scarpe. Having telephoned Brigade and asked for artillery to be brought to bear on them, they were told it was beyond the range of the guns.

The German units may have been beyond range of the British guns but the Northamptons were not beyond the range of German guns, as they discovered when the whole battalion came under heavy artillery fire. At 3.15pm the shelling increased on the Bois de la Ville [Maroeuil Wood] and on the B and D Company localities. Captain Houchin takes up the story:

> *The OC A Company, in the wood, was a very well known officer amongst the younger senior officers, popular, very social; he was a magnificent cricketer, an army hockey player, an excellent tennis player and a great personality. But he always exaggerated, it was a joke with us, he exaggerated everything ... when he went into the wood he was full of apprehension, and though the Adjutant*

went down to see him, he would not dig in. When the German artillery fire opened the effect in the woods was that the shells burst in the tops of the trees. This completely unnerved the company commander, who left his company and was picked up by the Quartermaster, two miles back. He was brought forward to the company and replaced in command of his company.

But the damage had already been done, the men of A Company began streaming out of the wood and the Germans took full advantage, inflicting heavy casualties on the Northamptons. The officer in question was Captain Robert Melsome and some urgent action was required if the situation was to be contained. Responding quickly, Lieutenant Colonel Hinchliffe replaced A Company with Captain Alexander Norman's C Company, who had been in reserve. This apparent blip on Melsome's career appeared not to hinder his subsequent promotion and, although he was captured on the Ypres-Comines

A young Captain Robert Melsome, taken when he was a second lieutenant.

Canal seven days later, he retired as a brigadier in 1961. During the night D Company was attacked and the enemy gained a foothold in Maroeuil village; a swift counter-attack by two platoons at dawn on 23 May restored the status quo and the attackers withdrew. But this was just the beginning. Captain Houchin described the next move by the enemy:

Artillery fire on the area increased as the day went on and during the early morning we saw German tanks, sixteen of them, and two hundred infantry, advancing across the open ground towards Maroeuil Wood. The German tanks arrived first and one was knocked out by an anti-tank gun. Another tank didn't come on as far but the OC [officer commanding] B Company got the old Boys rifle into action, got direct hits and all the tanks withdrew. The German infantry then got through the wood and had a battle with C Company, who suffered heavy casualties. Finally C Company was completely overrun.

Two platoons from the Seaforth Highlanders' D Company, under the command of 23-year-old Second Lieutenant Peter Fleming, were sent to support the Northamptons, but were not seen again, the war diary simply recording that a number of them were taken prisoner. One of those captured was Peter Fleming, who died of his wounds three days later and is buried at Cambrai (Route de Solesmes) Communal Cemetery.

Meanwhile, on the left flank Major Morrison and the Royal Scots Fusiliers arrived at 10.30am in the outskirts of Arras, having been harassed by an almost constant air attack. Fortunately we have Lieutenant Livingstone Bussell's diary account of his short stay at Ste-Catherine, from which it is possible to gain an insight into the confusion that presented itself to the battalion when they arrived. Bussell was second in command of D Company and although his account is at odds with the battalion war diary regarding the time of the battalion's arrival, he does say the company 'took up a position on the edge of a stream' near

Lieutenant Livingstone Bussell.

the Ste-Catherine bridge. This we can assume was the River Scarpe, which at this point is not much wider than a stream:

> *The village church and surrounding buildings had been completely smashed up. A few refugees were strolling about, both men and women. Difficult to know what to do with them as I was sure several of them were fifth columnists ... I had a few hours sleep in a very comfortable bed. One of the few nights that we were able to put on our pyjamas.*

Life here was reasonably tranquil compared to the pounding the Northamptons and Seaforth Highlanders were receiving further west along the valley. Lieutenant Colonel Hinchliffe's difficulties were exacerbated by the withdrawal of the French from Mont-St-Eloi on 23 May, leaving the enemy to gain a foothold in Bois de la Ville, circumstances which prompted Brigadier Stopford to seek permission for the brigade to withdraw to the line of the Arras-Béthune road. But it was easier said than done. The Northamptons and Seaforths ran the gauntlet of fire under a barrage of shelling and Stuka bombing attacks. Three companies of Northamptons managed the two mile move. C Company either failed to receive the order to move or were surrounded in the wood before they could withdraw. Whatever the case, Captain Alexander Norman and the survivors were taken prisoner. Captain Houchin remembered the orders arriving at D Company Headquarters:

> *At 6.00pm we got the orders to withdraw to Neuville-St-Vaast as fast as possible. [Lt Col Hinchliffe] pulled out A Company and Battalion HQ, and a motorcyclist came down to me in the village and told me I had to double back. I collected the platoons together,*

we ran up the road and came out into the open. I looked to my right and the whole of the wood was a blaze of tracer bullets, which owing to the trajectory fortunately just passed over the top of our heads.

The Northamptons suffered badly, recording over 350 casualties, a number which included Lieutenant Colonel Hinchliffe, Major J R Wetherall, the battalion's second in command, Captain Percy Green, the battalion Adjutant and Regimental Sergeant Major Goodall. The Royal Scots Fusiliers received their orders to move at 3.00am on 24 May but not before they had been on the receiving end of a heavy air raid. Livingstone Bussell recalled how he was strafed by a German aeroplane as he walked down the road towards Company HQ and later it was reported that Major Francis Adamson, commanding A Company, had been wounded, along with Second Lieutenant Ian McDavid. 'We were very relieved to move out', remarked Livingstone Bussel in his diary.

Casualties
The 6/Seaforth Highlanders lost heavily and, apart from the two platoons under the command of Peter Fleming from D Company, they also lost men in air attacks. The battalion does not draw attention to casualties in the war diary but a total of one hundred, killed and wounded would not be far short of the truth. We know the Northants suffered badly and by the time they arrived on the Ypres-Comines Canal two days later they were at little more than half strength. The Royal Scots Fusiliers were one of the few battalions in 17 Brigade that arrived in France with pretty much a full complement of officers and men. Despite the fact that they appear to have avoided the fighting that the Northamptons and Seaforths were involved with further west, they still recorded a steady stream of casualties from shelling and bombing over the course of 22/23 May.

Cemeteries
Anzin-St-Aubin Churchyard is on the D341, situated at an obvious crossroads. There is parking available on the left almost immediately after turning right at the crossroads, which is signposted Anzin-St-Aubin British Cemetery. You will find a row of five headstones to the right of the entrance, two of which are unidentified. In many ways the graves of **Private Thomas Bremner** and **Sergeant Archie Murdock** remain the only evidence that the Seaforth Highlanders and Royal Scots Fusiliers fought here in 1940. The third casualty, **Gunner Moses Brooks**, from 208/Battery, 52/Anti-Tank Regiment, was killed on 23 May, probably during the chaotic withdrawal of 17 Brigade.

Anzin-St-Aubin Churchyard Cemetery.

Anzin-St-Aubin British Cemetery is another 200 yards further along the road from where you parked to visit Anzin-St.Aubin Churchyard. There are four casualties here who died or were killed before 10 May 1940, the most senior and youngest being 26-year-old **Captain Dennis South** (5.A.3) of the 2/Hampshires, who was killed riding a motorcycle on 13 January 1940. He had just got married before the battalion left for France. Of the remaining three men, 43-year-old **Private Albert Crossland** (5.A.4) and **Driver Frederick Lane** (5.A.1) were both serving with the RAOC and **Sergeant Alfred Randall** (5.A.5) was serving with 4/Anti-Aircraft Regiment.

Maroeuil Communal Cemetery is best approached from the D341, north of the village. As you approach Maroeuil, which is on your left, you will pass over three crossroads; at the fourth turn left along a narrow minor road which, after the left hand bend, becomes Rue de Fresnoy. The cemetery is 100 yards further along on the left and should not be confused with Maroeuil British Cemetery, which is at the end of a track running

The entrance to Maroeuil Communal Cemetery.

off Rue de Stade. There is plenty of parking near the French National Cemetery. Enter the communal cemetery and go straight ahead until you see the **Tombe Famille Galvaire**, turn right here and you will see the CWGC plot by the east wall. There are now thirty-five casualties of the Second World War, of which three are unidentified. This plot should be renamed the Northamptonshire Cemetery as every one of the identified men are from the 2/Northamptons, many of them probably from C Company. We can assume that the three unidentified are also from the same battalion. Irish born 23-year-old **Second Lieutenant Herbert Oswald** was a graduate of Keble College Oxford and was killed on 23 May while serving with C Company. Tragically, his younger brother, Noel, died in April 1942 whilst serving as an officer cadet in the Royal Engineers. **Lance Corporal Wilfred Leach** was 32-years-old when he was killed at Maroeuil and buried, with a number of his mates, in Mme Leclercq's garden on Rue de la Marliere, before being reinterred in the communal cemetery. A former regular soldier, he was recalled to the colours in June 1939 and was last seen by his wife and family while on leave in February 1940. The cemetery is a lasting remembrance to the stand of the Northamptons. Before you leave it is worth spending a few minutes in the French Military Cemetery, where there are 585 casualties of the First World War, including the two sons of Général d'Armau de Pouydraguin, who commanded the French 47th Division between March

1915 and 1917. **Sous Lieutenant Jacques d'Armau de Pouydraguin** (Row 1 Grave 2) and his younger brother, **Sous Lieutenant Augustin d'Armau de Pouydraguin,** who is buried next to him, were killed in May 1915. You will also see a monument erected to commemorate the 156th and 160 Infantry Regiments. Inaugurated in May 1919, it was financed by the parents of **Commandant Georges Lilleman** (Row 2 Grave 109), who was killed at La Targette in May 1915.

Mont-St-Eloi Communal Cemetery is north of the village, behind the ruins of the former Mont-St- Eloi Abbey, which is classified as an historic monument and is an outstanding landmark that can be seen for miles around. The 12/Lancers had an observation post here. There is only one unidentified casualty amongst the five headstones of men from 208/Battery, 52/Anti-Tank Regiment. Their deaths, on 22 May 1940, were the result of a 'friendly fire' incident when French tanks were engaged in error near Berthonval Farm.

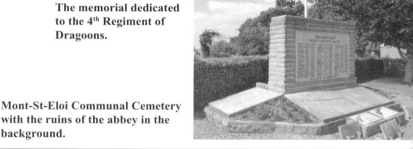

The memorial dedicated to the 4th Regiment of Dragoons.

Mont-St-Eloi Communal Cemetery with the ruins of the abbey in the background.

Chapter Seven

Conclusions

One has to question the apparent confusion that surrounded the Frankforce operation. On one hand Gort was clearly considering the possibility of striking into the flank of the panzer corridor as part of a joint counter-attack with the French; while, on the other, Franklyn tells us he was unaware of any wider strategic implications. Even after Franklyn was informed by the 12/Lancers of the weight of German armour in the area, he still continued with his original brief to clear the area south of Arras of 'weak German forces'. Two questions immediately arise from this state of affairs: Why did Franklyn not seek further clarification from Gort and why did Gort choose not to inform Franklyn of his intentions? What is equally disturbing is that information received on 21 May, regarding the destruction of 70 Brigade and the contact between the 12/Lancers and a German armoured column on the Arras-St Pol road, was not passed on to 151 Brigade.

Further issues inevitably arise over the matter of command. Who, historians have asked, was in command on 21 May? Franklyn had delegated command to Major General Martel, Brigadier Churchill informed the infantry commanding officers that they were the column commanders and Brigadier Pratt, commanding 1/Tank Brigade, told his commanding officers they were only in support of the infantry and *not* under their command. To make matters even more confusing, Brigadier Vyvyan Pope was present during the early part of the battle issuing orders from his staff car, as was his boss, Major General Martel. The late Professor Richard Holmes made the taciturn point that Rommel may have been

Brigadier Douglas Pratt gained his experience of tanks as a company commander at Cambrai in 1917.

In 1940 Brigadier Vyvyan Pope was attached to GHQ as Director of Armoured Fighting Vehicles.

commanding from too far forward, but the British commanders were perhaps too far back to be effective.

Another misconception was that the attack was a joint operation between infantry and armour; nothing can be further from the truth. There was no training between infantry and armour and, for the huge majority of the Durhams, the 21 May was the first occasion that they had even seen a tank. Encouraging the columns to advance quickly had only one outcome, that of armour and infantry becoming separated from the outset of the attack; a notion exacerbated by non-existent communication within the British armoured columns and between armour and infantry. Karl-Heinz Frieser in his book *The Blitzkrieg Legend* is damming in his criticism of the British attack, writing that the only command system used by the British was 'attacking by instinct'. British officers were often forced to either dismount from their tanks or lead by hand signals with their hatches open, circumstances which accounted for the deaths of Lieutenant Colonels Heyland at Wailly and Fitzmaurice below Telegraph Hill. The loss of direction by 7/RTR can be largely attributed to poor communication and the sense of urgency that cloaked the battlefield.

Basil Liddel Hart was equally critical of the failure of 21 May and cited three principal reasons: little infantry support, less artillery support and no air support. The lack of British air support and their failure to detect German armoured formations in the area is, of course, true; but what is equally surprising is the *Luftwaffe's* failure to identify the British columns as they moved south from Vimy Ridge.

Some 452 Hurricane fighters were sent to France in 1940 as part of the Air Component, of which only sixty-six returned. Between 10 and 20 May approximately 193 aircraft, mainly Fairy Battles and Blenheims, from the Advanced Air Striking Force, were lost to enemy action.

The French units operating on the right of the attack were clearly functioning under a cloud of confusion and, although dealt a harsh hand by British histories of the attack, did in fact offer valuable assistance, particularly to the Durhams in Wailly. They were also involved in an engagement with the 25th Panzer Regiment around Haute-Avenses and Agnez-lès-Duisans, which again is given very little credibility in British accounts. Given that they were seen as an 'add on' to the British attack and not kept informed of British movements, it is of little wonder that there were occasions of friendly fire reported between British and French units.

Another surprising aspect of the armoured clash at Arras was the air of invincibility that surrounded the panzer divisions in 1940. German tanks were, to a large extent, lightly armoured and under-gunned, the Panzer I and II in particular performing badly against their British and French counterparts; what set them apart from their allied opponents was their superior organization and command. When the French Somua S35 was first demonstrated in 1935 it was, arguably, one of the finest armoured vehicles in the world and was the first tank to incorporate an all-cast turret and hull. Yet, by 1942 the *Panzerwaffe* had not only caught up with the Allies in terms of tank design, but had overtaken them with tanks five to six times heavier and with a considerable increase in firepower.

However, despite its shortcomings and failure, the counter-stroke still achieved the essential element of surprise and caused widespread alarm amongst the German command. Perhaps a less hurried departure from the assembly area at Vimy would have produced a much heavier blow, although it should be said that the attack did hit Rommel's 7th Panzer Division at precisely the moment when his armoured units were ahead of the infantry and gunners. As for the infantry, they fought well given the uncertainties of the day; both the Durham battalions were fortunate that their commanding officers and senior NCOs were men who had already fought in one conflict and possessed the determination to rally their less experienced junior ranks and fight on regardless. Such was the case with the two tank battalions, although sadly they lost both their commanding officers and over half the tanks that went into the engagement.

The attack did enable the British to tighten their hold on Arras – albeit temporarily – and, as is often cited, built doubts in the minds of German High Command as to the speed of their advance and generated the subsequent Hitler halt order of 24-27 May. While this may not be completely accurate, after the war von Rundstedt admitted that the Arras counter-stroke came at a critical moment and 'for a short time it was

The German infantry soldier of May 1940. The soldier on the left is carrying two stick grenades and is armed with a Mauser Kar98k bolt action rifle. The *Gefreiter* on the right is armed with an MP40 Sub-Machine gun.

feared the panzer divisions would be cut off before the infantry divisions could come up to support them'. The delay imposed by the Frankforce counterstroke certainly allowed reinforcements to be shipped over to Boulogne on 22 May – a lesson that was repeated at Calais – postponing the move of three panzer divisions towards Dunkerque until 27 May; by which time a more robust defence of the port had been organized to cover the evacuation. In checking the German advance it also added a vital twenty-four hours to the time available for the fortification and defence of the Canal Line. Most historians agree that the so-called miracle of Dunkerque may have had its foundations laid at Arras on 21 May 1940, but the author is of the opinion that the real miracle – if indeed we can use such an emotive term – was the result of the host of desperate rearguard actions that culminated with the Dunkerque evacuation. The account of the defence of Cassel and Hazebrouck can be read in the Battleground Europe publication *Cassel and Hazebrouck 1940*.

Even after ordering Arras to be abandoned, Gort still remained faithful to the notion of an allied attack across the Somme, an operation he withdrew from after it became apparent that the French contribution would only be one division. Disappointment did not rest there, as yet more disturbing news arrived at GHQ announcing the collapse of the Belgian front at Courtrai and the German Sixth Army's push towards Ypres, thus threatening to cut off any proposed evacuation route left to the BEF. Gort's dispatch of the 5th and 50th Divisions to the line of the Ypres-Comines Canal, was, in the opinion of many historians, the act that saved the BEF from total destruction.

As we know, on 22 May the German divisions continued to by-pass Arras, the 5th Panzer Division moving north to Souchez and the 20th Motorized Division making for Vimy Ridge, while the 12th Infantry Division prepared to cross the River Scarpe between Athies and Roeux. The 5th Panzer Division advance north was delayed by 7/RTR on the Lorette spur, an action in which 46-year-old Major Hugh Garret, their new commanding officer, was killed. He is buried, along with six others, in Avion Communal Cemetery, Lens. Eventually, on the morning of 24 May units of the 5th Panzer Division and the 12th Infantry Division met on Vimy Ridge. It would be another four years before British troops were back in possession of Vimy Ridge and Arras.

Chapter Eight

The Tours

There are three car tours that take in the 70 Brigade calamity of the 20 May and the Frankforce attack of 21 May and, while I have not included maps for these tours [the IGN Série Bleu 1:25000 maps are more than sufficient], all three offer the battlefield visitor the opportunity to engage in short walks. Space has precluded any car tours along the Scarpe valley, but again, these two areas are relatively simple to explore using IGN Série Bleu 1:25000 maps. However, I have drawn maps for the two walking routes, which allow the visitor to explore central Arras and the northern defences controlled by the Welsh Guards at St-Nicolas and Ste-Catherine. In addition, there is a short guide to other sites of interest in Arras, which include the Citadel, Wellington Quarry and the two military cemeteries. Much of the area covered by the guide is dotted with cafés and other refreshment venues. The author strongly suggests obtaining a street map of Arras from the Tourist Office to supplement these excursions. Nonetheless, this is northern France, so be prepared as the weather can demand a more prudent use of waterproof clothing and walking boots when venturing off the beaten track.

Maps

As mentioned above, the tours described in this book are best supported by the IGN Série Bleu 1:25000 maps, which can be purchased at most good tourist offices, in the bigger local supermarkets and online from www.mapsworldwide.com. Arras is covered by IGN 2406E and the area east of the city by 2406O. However, bear in mind that satellite navigation can be a very useful supplement in supporting general route finding, particularly when trying to locate obscure CWGC cemeteries and navigating the streets of Arras. The Michelin Travel Partner Map can also be downloaded free onto your iPad, which is also very useful for consulting Google Earth or *Geoportail*, the French equivalent.

Travel and where to stay

By far the quickest passage across the Channel is via the Tunnel at Folkstone, the thirty six minutes travelling time comparing favourably with the longer ferry journey from Dover to Calais or Dunkerque. Travelling times vary according to traffic; but as a rough guide the journey from Calais to Arras via the A26 is about an hour, while Dunkerque to Arras takes some twenty-five minutes longer. Whether your choice of route is over or under the Channel, early booking is always recommended if advantage is to be taken of the cheaper fares. If you are intending to base yourself in Arras the author can recommend the four-star **Hotel Mercure** near the railway station, which is situated on the Boulevard Carnot. The hotel has the advantage of an underground car park and a bar and offers excellent accommodation. The author further suggests that the cafe at the nearby railway station is a good venue for a light breakfast. There are numerous other hotels in the city which come with recommendations, including the three-star **Hotel Ibis Arras Centre les Places** in the Place d'Ipswich, which is much closer to the Place de Héros and Palais-St-Vaast. For those of you who wish a more outdoor experience, *Camping la Paille Haute*, at Boiry-Notre-Dame, is just over six miles from Arras and offers mobile homes to rent and has the advantages of a heated swimming pool. As always, there is a plethora of bed and breakfast and self catering accommodation available on the internet and, for those of you who prefer a more rural location, the gite, *Le Clos du Carpediem*, at Cambligneul, is excellent. It is eight miles north of Arras and situated in a gated farm complex. The owner can be contacted by telephone on: 00 33 (0) 3 21 71 18 62 and Mobile: 00 33 (0) 6 62 37 41 47 or by email: stolat@live.fr .Further information on all aspects of accommodation can be obtained from the Tourist Office in Arras situated in the Place des Héros. Their address is: Hôtel de Ville, Place des Héros, 62000 Arras, or email: contact@explorearras.com

Driving
Driving abroad is not the expedition it was years ago and most battlefield visitors these days may well have already made the journey several times. However, if this is the first time you have ventured on French and Belgian roads there are one or two common sense rules to take into consideration. Ensure your vehicle is properly insured and covered by suitable breakdown insurance; if in doubt contact your insurer, who will advise you. There are also a number of compulsory items to be carried by motorists that are required by French law. These include your driving licence and vehicle registration documents, a warning triangle, a *Conformité Européenne* (CE) approved fluorescent safety vest for each person travelling in the car, headlamp beam convertors and the visible display of a GB plate. Whereas some modern cars have built in headlamp convertors and many have a GB plate incorporated into the rear number

plate, French law also requires the vehicle to be equipped with a first aid kit and a breath test kit. If you fail to have these available there are some hefty on the spot fines for these motoring offences if caught driving without them. Most, if not all, of these items can be purchased at the various outlets at the Tunnel, the channel port at Dover and on board the ferries themselves.

Driving on the 'wrong side of the road' can pose some challenges. Here are three tips that the author has always found useful:

1. When driving on single carriageway roads try to stop at petrol stations on the right hand side of the road. It is much more natural then to continue driving on the right hand side of the road after you leave. Leaving a garage or supermarket is often the time when you find yourself naturally turning onto the wrong side of the road.
2. Take your time! Don't rush! If you rush your instinct may take over and your instinct is geared to driving on the left.
3. Pay particular care on roundabouts. A lot of drivers do not or rarely appear to use indicators. Navigators remember to look at the signs anti-clockwise and drivers remember that the danger is coming from the left.

On a more personal note it is always advisable to ensure that your E111 Card is valid in addition to any personal accident insurance you may have; and have a supply of any medication that you may be taking at the time.

Visiting Commonwealth War Graves Commission Cemeteries
The cemeteries visited in this guide are all generally in churchyards or in communal cemeteries such as **Arras Communal Cemetery,** although you will find British casualties from 1940 located in a number of existing First World War Cemeteries, such as **Bucquoy Road British Cemetery** at Ficheux and **Habarcq Communal Cemetery Extension.** When visiting the fallen from the Second World War in and around Arras, it is impossible not to be constantly reminded of casualties from the First World War, the numbers of which probably horrified the men of the BEF who fought in this area during May 1940. The visitor will also come across the graves of aircrew that were shot down over the course of the war and those men who died during the advance in 1944 after the D-Day landings. The graves of men killed in the area during May 1940 are probably the least visited in the whole of France; the small numbers of men, whose headstones are almost lost amongst the French civilians in communal cemeteries, are all but forgotten. Not every small communal

cemetery in the area has been visited and those such as Arleux-en-Gohelle and Thélus Communal Cemeteries, to the north of Arras, have been excluded, along with some others, because they are outside the general area of this book. Visitors to the area should ensure that these soldiers and airmen are not ignored and make a point of visiting their often isolated graves. A list of cemeteries where the casualties of 1940 are buried can be found in Appendix 2.

The concept of the Imperial War Graves Commission (IWGC) was created by Major Fabian Ware, the volunteer leader of a Red Cross mobile unit that saw service on the Western Front for most of the period of the First World War. Concern for the identification and burial of the dead led him to begin lobbying for an organization devoted to burial and maintenance of those who had been killed or died in the service of their country. This led to the Prince of Wales becoming the president of the IWGC in May 1917, with Ware as his vice president. Forty-three years later the IWGC became the Commonwealth War Graves Commission (CWGC). The commission was responsible for introducing the standardized headstone, which brought equality in death regardless of rank, race or creed and it is this familiar white headstone that you will see now in CWGC cemeteries all over the world. Where there is a CWGC plot within a communal or churchyard cemetery the familiar green and white sign at the entrance, with the words *Tombes de Guerre du Commonwealth* will indicate their presence. French military cemeteries are usually marked by the French national flag and, those

The familiar green and white sign denotes CWGC headstones are present in the cemetery.

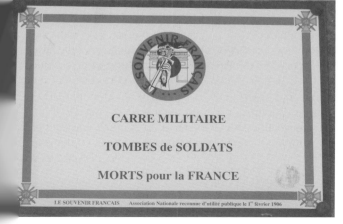

French Military plots within communal cemeteries are usually marked with the blue and red bordered sign with the words *Carre Militaire, Tombes de Soldats, Morts pour la France.*

which are contained within communal cemeteries are often marked by a sign at the cemetery entrance bearing the words: *Carre Militaire, Tombes de Soldats, Morts pour la France.*

Arras

By the end of the First World War Arras was in ruins and for almost three years, from October 1914 to April 1917, the inhabitants of the city lived below ground under the almost continual shelling of the German artillery. The British front line was just east of the city and by the end of the war only five percent of the houses in the city were habitable; Saint-Vaast Abbey, together with much of the remaining architectural heritage in the city was completely destroyed. During May 1940 the city was again badly damaged but, although there was considerable destruction from German aerial bombing, the damage was not on the same scale as that of twenty-three years earlier.

After the conclusion of the First World War, the French Government decided that faithful reproductions of these ancient buildings should be built in their original locations as a tribute to the city's medieval heritage. Thus the chief architect responsible for France's national monuments, **Pierre Paquet** (1875-1959), was given the formidable task of rebuilding Arras from a mass of rubble. Using photographs and archive documents, Paquet designed facades faithful to the spirit of the original buildings while ensuring the interiors were built to modern specifications. Apart from the main monuments and historical buildings, the city was largely rebuilt in the Art Deco style, which is most visible on many of the house facades along Rue Gambetta, Rue Ernestale and Place du Théâtre. If you are staying in Arras for a few days then it may be worthwhile investing in an Arras City Pass, which gives favourable discounts at a number of the attractions in the city, including the Wellington Quarry, the Belfry tower and the Museum of Fine Arts. Details can be obtained from the Tourist Office.

Since 1945 the population of the city has increased by over 10,000 and the city boundaries have been extended considerably by private housing and the development of the industrial base. Many of the previously separate villages that lay outside the city boundaries have now been absorbed and it can often be difficult to pin-point exactly where you are.

Today restaurants and shops abound and the city offers attractive breaks for the tourist and, although the emphasis is on the legacy of the First World War, there is still much to see from the short occupation by British forces in 1940.

Market days
Place des Héros: every Wednesday and all day on Saturday. Grand Place: all day on Saturday, resulting in no parking on that day. Place de la Vacquerie: all day on Saturday.

Other Arras visits
Both the Faubourg d'Amiens, the Arras Flying Services Memorial and the Citadel are to be found on Boulevard du Général de Gaulle and can be accessed by the local *Citadine* bus service that tours the city. The service is free and buses run every five minutes, details of which can be gained from the tourist office. Alternatively, you can use your vehicle and park in the lay-by on Avenue du Mémorial des Fusillés, just next to the cemetery.

The Faubourg d'Amiens
The British and Commonwealth section of the cemetery was begun in March 1916, and continued to be used by field ambulances and fighting units until November 1918. The cemetery was enlarged after the Armistice when graves were brought in from the battlefields and from two smaller cemeteries in the vicinity. Today the cemetery contains over 2,650 burials of the First World War, ten of which are unidentified.

The eight Second World War burials, of which one is unidentified, are located along the southern wall in Plot VIII near to the Cross of Sacrifice. None of these men were killed in 1940. **Flight Sergeant Clifford Turl** (Pilot), **Sergeant Patrick Whelton** (Navigator) and **Sergeant John Butler** (Wireless Operator/Air Gunner) were the crew of a Boston that was shot down after attacking the steel and armament works at Denain on 16 August 1943. **Aircraftman Second Class Alfred Blagdon** was killed on 16 September 1944 while **Lieutenant Francis Simpson** was drowned near Menin on 7 September 1944. Two men who died on the same day in September 1944 were **Private William Tate** and **Sergeant Donald Wigley-Jones.** Unusually for a British and Commonwealth cemetery, there is a special memorial to **Colonel Thomas Christian** of the 361st Fighter Group, USAAF, who was killed flying his P-51 Mustang during a bombing raid on the railway marshalling yards at Arras on 12 August 1944. Amongst the myriad of First World War headstones is that of **Captain Arthur Colthurst** (1.H.14) of the 15/Gloucester Regiment, who was killed in action on 25 October 1916. His youngest son, 33-year-old **Flying Officer John Colthurst**, was killed in action while serving as a bomb aimer with 115 Squadron on 24 February 1944. His body was never recovered and is now commemorated on the Runnymede Memorial. John Colthurst was

The Faubourg d'Amiens and the Arras Flying Services Memorial are on Boulevard du Général de Gaulle.

six years old when his father was killed in action. His eldest son, 42-year-old **Commander Anthony Colthurst** RN, was killed whilst in command of HMS *Avenger* in November 1942 when she was sunk by U-155. Only twelve of the crew survived. His name is commemorated on the Lee-on-Solent Memorial.

The adjacent **Arras Memorial** commemorates almost 35,000 servicemen from the United Kingdom, South Africa and New Zealand who died in the Arras sector between the spring of 1916 and 7 August 1918 and have no known grave. The **Arras Flying Services Memorial** commemorates some 1,000 airmen of the Royal Naval Air Service, the Royal Flying Corps, and the Royal Air Force, who were killed on the Western Front and who have no known grave. The observant will notice the memorial commemorates some very well known names, **Major 'Mick' Mannock, Lieutenant Arthur Rhys-Davids** and **Captain Douglas Bell**, to mention but three!

Just next to the entrance you will see Avenue du Mémorial des Fusillés, which leads through the Bois de Citadel to the site – **Mur des Fusillés** – where the German garrison executed French resistance prisoners during the Second World War. Civilian opposition to the German occupation in the Arras area was relentless and 218 of the resistance fighters were executed in the ditch of the Vauban fortress. After you pass through the metal gates and turn the corner, the replacement

The entrance to the Mur des Fusillés.

The execution post stands amidst the names of the resistance fighters who died in this sombre place.

execution post and the names of the dead, which are on the surrounding walls, make this an altogether sombre spot.

The Citadel

Retrace your steps to Faubourg d'Amiens and turn right. The entrance to the Citadel is 280 yards further down the road and can be accessed by walking across the bridge which spans the moat. The Citadel was built under the plans of **Sébastien de Vauban** between 1668 and 1672 on the orders of Louis XIV (1661-1715). The aim of the Citadel was to protect the city from attacks but was rapidly nicknamed 'the beautiful useless' because of its position, which was hardly strategic! The Citadel houses the oldest surviving chapel in the city: the Chapel Saint Louis, dating from the 17th century and, from April to October, the Salle des Familles hosts an exhibition presenting the history of the Citadel. Up until July 2009 the Citadel was home to the 601st Infantry Regiment but after is disbandment the Citadel was sold to Arras for what had been described as 'a token sum'. Entrance is free, apart from the restrictions from mid June to mid July (details from the Tourist Office). Tank enthusiasts will

The entrance to the Citadel.

be interested to know that during the build up to the April 1917 offensive tanks were kept hidden from enemy view in the ditches surrounding the Citadel, camouflaged underneath netting. After leaving the Citadel you have a choice of either returning on the free bus service or, by walking through the Jardin des Allées, to return to the Grand Place.

The Jardin des Allées is opposite the Citadel.

The Wellington Quarry

Although more associated with the First World War and the 1917 Battles of Arras, the quarry is worth a visit if you have time and is ideal for a rainy day! Situated on **Rue Arthur Delétoille**, the quarry is in effect part of an underground town where more than 20,000 British and Dominion soldiers gathered before the attack on the German lines was opened on 9 April 1917. There is free parking and tours last about one hour. The quarry is open all year round from 10.00am to 6.00pm, with an hour's break for lunch beginning at 12.30pm. Full price is currently €6.90, with the concessionary rate at €3.20. Tickets can also be purchased online from the website or, alternatively, at the Arras Tourist Office. http://www.explorearras.com/fr/visiter/carriere-wellington.

Walk 1

Arras Central

Start: This circular route starts and finishes at Place du Maréchal Foch (Station Square) and visits central Arras taking the visitor to a mixture of famous buildings and sites associated with the First and Second World Wars.
Distance : Two miles

There is plenty of parking in **Place du Maréchal Foch**, although much of it will incur a small cost. Our walk begins by the magnificent French War Memorial, ❶ which commemorates the dead and missing from both world wars as well as those from the wars in Korea and Indo-China. Walking round the memorial you will notice a plaque commemorating

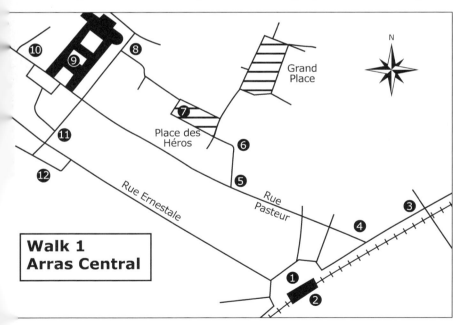

A simplified map of central Arras showing the circular route beginning at Place du Maréchal Foch.

The rebuilt railway station which was opened in 1957.

those who were killed and injured in the attack of 19 May 1940. The railway station ❷ was first opened in 1898 and badly damaged during the First World War. Repaired between 1919 and 1920, it was damaged again in May 1940, with the most devastating air raid taking place on 19 May. The station square was the scene of the horrific encounter had by **Second Lieutenant Tony Younger** when he came across a refugee carrying the headless body of a young girl, a scene he says, that remained imprinted on his mind for years afterwards.

After the end of the war the decision was taken to build a new station on the site of the old building, a project that was realized in April 1957, when the new station that you see today was officially opened. It was from the railway station that the 'Station Rifles' were

The French War Memorial in Place du Maréchal Foch.

collected by **Captain Henry Dimsdale** on 17 May. After relieving No. 2 Company, Welsh Guards, on 21 May, the station square was occupied by No. 4 Company. The war diary tells us that:

11 Platoon were right forward in the square, 10 Platoon left forward and 12 Platoon in support. The take-over was completed by 12 noon and the Anti-Tank Platoon came under command. During the afternoon enemy aircraft were very active and at least three low flying machine gun attacks were vented on the company. 242 Company RE came in on our left rear and blocked the station footbridge.

Keeping the railway station building on your right, walk up **Rue de Douai** for 380 yards until you arrive at the girder bridge – **Pont St-Sauveur** - which carries the Avenue de Lattre de Tassigny ❸ over the railway line. This is the bridge which is described in the Welsh Guards war diary as being north of the railway station, it was held from 17 May by 1 Platoon and **Second Lieutenant Arthur Pearce-Serocold** (Prince of Wales Company). Their stay was not without drama, particularly on 19 May, when the station was bombed. Eight French civilian cars were commandeered to block the bridge on 20 May and the approaches were mined. Two refugee cars were subsequently blown up after detonating mines on the bridge, resulting in two refugees being killed. Pearce-Serocold was later killed in action in Tunisia in 1942. The bridge was also protected by one 257/Battery anti-tank gun from A Troop (Troop

Pont St-Sauveur.

125

Sergeant Major Neal), who had another positioned in station square. A platoon from the Northumberland Fusiliers took over on 22 May.

Retrace your steps until you reach Rue Pasteur **4** on your right. Turn west and walk along this road for a further 325 yards until you reach **Rue Wacquez Glasson 5** on the right. This pedestrian street leads directly to **Place de Ipswich**, which is dominated by the imposing **Église Saint Jean Baptist**, which took its name after Bishop de la Tour d'Auvergne, Bishop of Arras, made it his temporary cathedral in 1803. To the right of

Looking up Rue de la Housse towards the Église Saint Jean Baptist.

the entrance **6** is a plaque commemorating the bravery of **Warrant Officer Wacquez** and **Augustus Glasson**, two fire fighters who were killed in 1915 during the fire that 'ravaged' the church. Inside the church there are several artefacts which make a visit worthwhile and, apart from the Rubens painting depicting the descent of Christ from the cross, the altar and altar piece – both in marble - date from the 17th century and were part of the original chapel in the Petite Place [now Place des Héros] which was destroyed in 1792.

After leaving the church, walk directly ahead down **Rue de la Housse**, which leads into Place des Héros. This is the smaller of the two main squares in Arras and contains the Hôtel de Ville and the magnificent Belfry tower, which you can see ahead of you **7** at the end of the square.

On 8 October 1914 the Hotel de Ville, which dated from the 16th century, was

The entrance to Église Saint Jean Baptist.

burned to the ground by German incendiary shells. A fortnight later the Belfry tower, the pride of the city, collapsed. No one today would think that behind the medieval appearance of the Belfry tower lies a contemporary structure made of concrete and steel. The larger of the two squares – the Grand Place – is a short walk along the connecting **Rue de la Taillerie** and, like its smaller counterpart, is surrounded by shops and cafes.

As you walk towards the **Hôtel de Ville** in the Place des Héros, you will see the entrance to the Tourist Office, which is situated on the ground floor as you enter the building. To the right of the entrance is the memorial to the resistance fighters who lost their lives during the Second World War; it was the sacrifice of these men and women that prompted the Arras City fathers to rename the Petite Place in their honour, hence **Place des Héros**. The office is open every day of the year except Christmas Day and New Year's Day, but be aware that it is closed for lunch between 12.00 noon and 2.00pm. This is also the entrance to the limestone quarries that are a feature of underground Arras and referred to as the **Boves**. Tours cost €5.30, with a concessionary price of €3.10.

Looking across Place des Héros towards the Hôtel de Ville.

There are a maximum of twenty-five individuals allowed on each tour, which lasts about forty-five minutes. Departure information is available from the Tourist Office, from where information regarding the ascent of the Belfry tower is also available. Each tour to the top of the Belfry tower is restricted to nineteen individuals and costs €3. The views from the Belfry tower are first class.

After leaving the Hôtel de Ville, turn right and walk to the left of the building along Rue Jacques Carron, which will take you to the small square behind the Hôtel de Ville. This is **Place de la Vacquerie**. Walk diagonally across the square to the right to reach **Rue Neuve des Ardents** and then take the first left, down the narrow **Rue Désiré Bras**. From this point the great buttresses of the Cathedral, **Notre Dame de l'Assomption et St-Vaast**, can be seen at the far end, complete ❽ with a profusion of shrapnel marks. Walk down the street, turning right at the bottom to find the entrance to the cathedral on your left. The original building was begun in 1778 but was only completed after the French Revolution. Sadly, it was almost completely destroyed during the First World War and only

The cathedral as seen from Rue Désiré Bras. The buildings of Palais-St-Vaast can be seen on the left.

opened again in 1934. It survived the Second World War, suffering only from bomb damage in 1944. As you walk round the building you will notice the plaque to **Victor-Jean Perrin** (1894-1971) who was appointed Bishop of Arras in 1945. Perrin fought as a *lieutenant* in the First World War before he was ordained in 1921. He enlisted again in 1940 and fought the Germans at Rennes, where he refused to surrender. On the same column can be seen the memorial tablet to the British and Empire dead of the First World War; similar tablets can be found in cathedrals across northern France.

Leave the cathedral by the same entrance that you used to enter the building and retrace your steps past Rue Désiré Bras and follow the railings to the junction with **Rue Paul Doumer**. You are now walking alongside the Palais-St-Vaast, **❾** which you can see on your right. At the end of the street, turn right to the imposing entrance gates to **Palais-St-Vaast** courtyard. In May 1940, during the defence of Arras, these gates would have been guarded by soldiers of the Welsh Guards and Green Howards. This is where **Major General Petre** had his headquarters, in the cellars beneath the building; and where **Major Alan Coleman** first

The entrance to Palais-St-Vaast courtyard.

came to meet Petre and **Lieutenant Colonel Felix Copland-Griffiths** of the Welsh Guards. It is more than likely he would have driven through the entrance gates to the courtyard. Today, it is the entrance to the **Museum of Fine Arts**, which occupies a large section of Palais-St-Vaast and it well worth a visit. Opening times and entrance costs can be obtained from the Tourist Office, but it is worth remembering that entrance is free on the first Sunday of the month and on European Heritage days.

Leave Palais-St-Vaast and turn right to reach the entrance to the **Jardin de la Légion d'Honneur**. Just after you pass through the gates ❿ you will find two memorials on the left. The first is the Royal Tank Regiment Memorial and the second is the Welsh Guards' Memorial.

The Royal Tank Regiment memorial.

Both of these memorials relate to the 1940 battles and the occupation of Arras. After leaving the gardens by the same entrance, cross the road into **Place de la Madeleine,** from where the narrow **Rue Maximilien Robespierre** can be seen bending round to the left at the end of **Rue de la Gouvernance**. At No 9 is the house, which was built in 1730 and occupied by Robespierre from 1787 to 1789.

The memorial dedicated to the Welsh Guards.

Robespierre was executed in Paris in 1794. Today it is home to an exhibition retracing the history of the Journeymen Companions (Compagnonnage). The museum is open Tuesday to Friday, 2.00pm to 5.30pm and 2.30pm to 6.30pm at weekends and public holidays. From October to April it is closed on Wednesday and Friday. Admission is €2, children are free.

Continue to the end of the road which forms a junction with ⑪ **Place du Théâtre**. The theatre is almost directly opposite you. It was in this square, then called rather inappropriately **Place de Comédie**,that the guillotine was installed during the terror. From one of the theatre balconies it is said that the Pro-Consul, Joseph Le Bon, and his wife applauded the executions. More than 500 executions were carried out in this small square. Le Bon was himself executed in 1795 at Amiens. If you wish to visit the **Hôtel de Guînes** and step back into the 18th century, turn left and walk along **Rue des Jongleurs,** to find the building on your left. The courtyard is open every day and the building, which was built in 1738 as the residence of the de Guînes family, is open from April to September.

From the theatre, turn right and cross over **Rue Ernestale** and almost straight in front of you is the narrow **Rue du Petite Chaudron**, leading to **Rue du College.** Turn left to find the **Hôtel de l'Univers** ⑫ on your right. The rebuilt hotel was hit on the night of 14/15 May during an air

The Hôtel de l'Univers is tucked away in Rue du College.

raid that is said to have specifically targeted the building where British officers were billeted and attributed to fifth column activity. Headquarters staff from GHQ and several newspaper correspondents were lodged in the hotel, which was also a press centre where a daily press briefing took place each day. **Bernard Gray** of the *Daily Mirror* remembered the hotel for 'its extraordinarily bad service' and 'bedrooms as cold as the attitude of the management'. Avoiding the carnage that night was **Henry, Duke of Gloucester**, who had driven to meet the King of the Belgians at a secret location, only to be caught up in the bombing at Tournai, where he was wounded. Several of the hotel's occupants were killed, including a number who had rooms next to the Duke. During the raid two bombs fell on the hotel and other buildings close by were badly damaged; amongst the dead were 26-year-old **Second Lieutenant John Hobson** from Leamington Spa and **Major William Scott.**

The 64-year-old **Brigadier Mainwaring Walsh,** who was a King's Messenger, was badly injured in the raid and died of his wounds the next day. All three men are buried at Avesnes-le-Comte Communal Cemetery Extension. One officer who had a narrow escape from the bombing was **Second Lieutenant John McSwiney,** who was on his way from Calais to rejoin his unit at Orthies. His attempt to find a room in the hotel was unsuccessful and he recalls wandering the streets of the city until the relative calm of the night was shattered by the bombing of the hotel. He still congratulates himself on a lucky escape. **Second Lieutenant Tony Younger** remembered being called out with his section of sappers to fight the fires in Arras that night and being directed to the Hôtel de l'Univers,

Second Lieutenant John Hobson was killed during the bombing of the Hôtel de l'Univers.

where he says seven people were killed. [Other sources place a much higher figure on the number of casualties.] It was burning so fiercely, he wrote, 'that there was little we could do'. Almost opposite the hotel is another narrow street that will take you back to meet **Rue Ernestale** again. Turn right and walk back to the station square and your vehicle.

Walk 2

St-Nicolas and Ste-Catherine

> **Start:** This circular route starts and finishes at the *Mairie* at St-Nicolas on Rue Aristide Briand. Visitors using satellite navigation should take note that there are two roads with the name Rue Aristide Briand, one of which is in the centre of Arras.
> **Distance:** Two miles

In 1940 Ste-Catherine and St-Nicolas were villages and districts to the north of Arras; Ste-Catherine lying to the west, and St-Nicolas to the east of the N37 to La Targette and Souchez. Today they have both merged into the greater conurbation of Arras and, to a great extent, lost their individual identities. This short walk begins outside the *Maire* at St-Nicolas, ❶ which is situated on the former roundabout where the Welsh

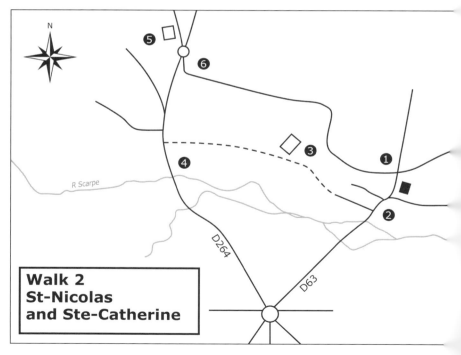

The Mairie at St-Nicolas.

Guards **Prince of Wales Company** were based during their stay in Arras. They arrived here at around 12.15pm via the St-Nicolas and Ste-Catherine bridges and established their headquarters in a garage on the roundabout. The Carrier Platoon, under the command of Lieutenant Dick Furness, was based nearby in the former Teclamite Service Garage. Later in the evening several vehicles were parked in the Renault Garage whose petrol pump became the petrol point for all the Welsh Guards' vehicles in the city. The area around the *Mairie* is now totally changed and the old buildings have largely been replaced by those you see now.

With the *Maire* behind you, walk down **Rue Raoul Briquet** past the church, crossing straight over the four-way staggered intersection into **Rue Anatole France**. The next road on the right is **Rue Marcel Sembat** and the house on the corner – Number 2 – was initially the temporary Welsh Guards Battalion Headquarters ❷ before it moved to Palais-St-Vaast. The house later became the Prince of Wales Company Officers Mess.

Rue Marcel Sembat is clearly marked.

Continue along **Rue Anatole France** for another seventy yards to the St-Nicolas bridge, which today is easily missed if travelling by car. The River Scarpe here is quite narrow and the

135

The building on the corner of Rue Marcel Sembat, which housed the Prince of Wales Company officers mess.

area surrounding it very different from May 1940. The bridge was initially held on 17 May by 22-year-old **Second Lieutenant Arthur Pearce-Serocold** and 1 Platoon (Prince of Wales Company) before they were relieved by one section of 11 Platoon from No. 4 Company, the war diary reporting that on 20 May **Captain Maurice Smart** had only four sections left under his command. It was across the bridges at St-Nicolas and Ste-Catherine that the Welsh Guards first entered Arras and it was over these bridges that the garrison left the city on the night of 23 May. Captain Maurice Smart's men also held the northern approaches and the road blocks on the bridge at Ste-Catherine with 12 Platoon. Later, one platoon from the 8/Northumberland Fusiliers, under **Second Lieutenant R Wilson,** reinforced the bridge at St-Nicolas and another, under **Second Lieutenant C H Mitchell**, strengthened the garrison at Ste-Catherine bridge. **Major Alan Coleman** in his diary account records 257/Battery leaving Arras using the bridge at St-Nicolas.

The bridge at St-Nicolas.

From the bridge retrace your steps to Rue Marcel Sembat and turn left to continue along the street to access the narrow **Voie des Croix**, which you will see directly ahead of you. This narrow pathway will take you to **St-Nicolas British Cemetery**. The cemetery ❸ contains no burials from the Second World War but there are several graves of

The entrance to the narrow Voie des Croix at the end of Rue Marcel Sembat.

interest, not least the four soldiers who were 'shot at dawn'. You will find these men in Plot II: **Private Norman Taysum** (II.C 16), **Private Thomas Ward** (II.C.17), **Private James Adamson** (II.C.18) and **Private Hector Dalande** (II.D.1). From March 1916 to the Armistice in 1918, the village of St-Nicolas was occupied by the BEF and for much of that time it was within the range of German artillery fire. The cemetery was started in March 1917 and used by the divisions and field ambulances stationed there until October 1918. The cemetery currently holds 364 burials, the majority of which are victims of the 1917 Battles of Arras.

Leave the cemetery and turn right, the pathway now becomes the **Chemin des 3 Fontaines** and will take you to the junction with the D341 in another 500 yards. Turn left to find the Ste-Catherine bridge ❹ 120 yards ahead of you. [There is another bridge 170 yards further along the road but this only spans a small tributary of the Scarpe.] The road block on the bridge was originally held by **PSM Albert Sanders** and the men of 12 Platoon, but Sanders and six of his men were killed during the early hours of 20 May when two bombs fell outside the 12 Platoon Headquarters. The surviving men of the platoon were placed under the command of **Lieutenant Sir Francis Winnington** and the dead were 'buried in a field near the bridge at Ste-Catherine'. Only **Guardsman**

St-Nicolas British Cemetery.

Lawrence Maxwell was later reinterred in Arras Communal Cemetery; the remaining men are all commemorated on the Dunkirk Memorial.

The bridge at Ste-Catherine was used by **Lieutenant Dick Furness** on the evening of 23 May, when he passed the Northumberland Fusilier guard post on his way to find a downed enemy airman. It was just north of the here that his carrier was hit by a shell fired from a British anti-tank gun, most probably from 257/Battery; the ensuing conversation was said to have been quite robust!

Just before you turn to retrace your steps, look across to your left along the Scarpe. The view is unfortunately largely obscured by buildings and trees, but this is where D Company of the Royal Scots Fusiliers were positioned and the area in which **Lieutenant Livingstone Bussell** wrote his diary account of D Company's stay in Arras.

Leave the bridge and continue past **Chemin des 3 Fontaines** on your right, from here the road ascends to a mini roundabout, at which point you should be able to see the walls of ❺ **Ste-Catherine Communal Cemetery** ahead of you on the left. There are seven identified Second World War casualties here and four unidentified, which are on the right as you enter the cemetery.

The mini roundabout at the top of Route de Lens with the communal cemetery on the left.

The only named 1940 casualty is **Private Alexander Frazer** of the 6/Seaforth Highlanders, who was killed on 21 May. The six Royal Air Force casualties were all crew members of the 582 Squadron Lancaster that crashed in the northwest suburbs of Arras on the night of 15/16 June 1944. 21-year-old **Pilot Officer Norman Tutt** (Pilot) is buried next to **Flight Sergeants Richard Harris** and **Harold Ames**, who share a headstone, as do **Flying Officer William Williams** and **Flight Sergeant Sidney Parr**. The seventh member of the crew, **Flight Sergeant F S Boots**, evaded capture and eventually returned to England. The three unidentified graves are in a separate plot immediately behind.

After leaving the cemetery turn right and retrace your steps to the roundabout, from where you will see **Rue des 4 Maisons** – signposted St-Nicolas – across the road on the left. This road, which bends round to the left ❻ after one hundred metres, was probably used by Dick Furness's Carrier Platoon as it patrolled the area between St-Nicolas and Ste-Catherine. A long road of some 600 yards, it runs parallel to the pathway you walked along between St-Nicolas and Ste-Catherine and runs between private houses before it bends round to the right into Rue Aristide Briand to return you to the *Mairie* at St-Nicolas.

Car Tour 1

The 70 Brigade Disaster

Start: The church at Neuville-Vitasse
Finish: Bucquoy Military Cemetery
Distance: Eight miles

This car tour follows the route taken by Brigadier Kircup's 70 Brigade from Neuville-Vitasse to Ficheux. We begin our route by the church and the village war memorial in Neuville-Vitasse. The war memorial is a rather splendid one and on the right hand panel are the civilian and military casualties of the Second World War. Mercifully, the village appears to have been spared the civilian atrocities committed by the *SS-Totenkopf* Division in Mercatel and other villages to the west of Arras.

The church and war memorial at Neuville-Vitasse.

The 1/Tyneside Scottish arrived in the village at 3.00am on 20 May 1940. The transport, under **Second Lieutenant James Dunn,** was immediately sent to Saulty to unload and return to Neuville-Vitasse at once. It is likely the battalion were under cover, as at dawn enemy aircraft began reconnoitring the village at low level and the war diary indicates that 'full concealment was practiced as previously ordered and no movement was allowed'. Before the battalion left the village **Staff Sergeant Perkins** and some 140 mixed RAOC and AMPC personnel, who appear to have been abandoned in the village, were taken under command. Many of these men were unarmed. At 7.00am **Lieutenant Colonel Swinburne** gave the orders for the battalion to move off to Saulty via Mercatel, Ficheux and Beaumetz. The village of Neuville-Vitasse was where **Captain George Harker** and the men of C Company were attacked shortly after Captain Esmond Adams and D Company had moved off towards Mercatel. C Company put up a spirited defence here but were overwhelmed.

Continue out of Neuville-Vitasse along the D34 until you reach the crossroads with the D917. It was from this vicinity that **Captain Esmond Adams** heard the noise of fighting coming from Neuville-Vitasse and returned with one platoon to offer assistance to George Harker's men if he could. At the crossroads go straight across and into the village of Mercatel, heading towards the church, where you will find the elaborate village war memorial commemorating the dead of the First World War. Continue for 200 yards and just before you reach the village green, look

The war memorial at Mercatel.

The village green at Mercatel takes its name from the events of 21 May.

Erected in 1975, the plaque commemorated the civilian dead murdered by the *SS-Totenkopf* Division.

up to the left to see a plaque on the wall of a private house. This plaque commemorates the civilian victims that were murdered by the *SS-Totenkopf* Division on 20 and 21 May 1940. The village green also takes its name from the events of 21 May. Continue straight ahead, turning left along **Rue Leauwette** for approximately 300 yards to where you will find **Mercatel Communal Cemetery** on the left. There is parking opposite the entrance. There are twenty casualties from May 1940 buried here, of which only seven are identified men who were serving with the Tyneside Scottish. The remaining unidentified headstones are more than likely to be men from the same battalion.

Mercatel Communal Cemetery.

Return to the village green and continue straight ahead along **Rue de la Chapelle**. The road bends round to the left to reach another small green on the right. Bear left, passing the green on the right and, at the fork in the road, take the right hand road towards Ficheux. At the point where you can see an electricity pylon, there is a single track road on the right. Park here. Ahead of you the road bends round to the left and, straight ahead, to the right of the road and across the fields, you can see the low roofs of some farm buildings. In May 1940 the road continued across the fields to the right of these buildings to a level crossing and the junction with the D919. We will visit the former level crossing later.

Continue straight on towards Ficheux and pass under two railway bridges to reach a crossroads. The coppice where A Company came under attack has long gone but the new road you have just travelled upon would have traversed through its northern edge. This was where **Lance Sergeant Richard Ogle** won his DCM after crawling out into the open under heavy fire to bring in a wounded man; he also recovered an abandoned Boys rifle, which he put to good use until he was taken prisoner. The fighting here was also graphically described by **CSM Charles Baggs**, who was eventually taken prisoner.

Turn right at the crossroads and drive for 200 yards uphill to the white house on the right. You will find the only remaining part of the former road a few yards beyond the house on the right. Park off the road as it can be quite busy. A plaque on the wall of the house, erected by André

The new crossroads with the D919. The village of Ficheux is straight across, while the Cagin family house and the former level crossing are to the right.

The house which once stood on the staggered crossroads close to the level crossing.

Coilliot, commemorates the men of the three 70 Brigade battalions who fell in this area on 20 May 1940. This is one of two buildings that stood here in May 1940 and was where HQ and B Company, Tyneside Scottish, arrived after Lieutenant Colonel Swinburne had detailed them to hold the road junction. The second building was demolished when the level crossing was removed as part of the construction of the new TGV railway line. Both these buildings were fortified by HQ Company, but set on fire by enemy shelling.

Erected by André Coilliot, the plaque commemorating the 70 Brigade encounter is a stark reminder of what occurred here in May 1940.

145

After D Company arrived at this point with **Captain Esmond Adams,** they advanced round the north side of, what has been described as a 'slight hill' towards Ficheux. One platoon of D Company, under the command of **Second Lieutenant Hunter**, advanced round the left flank towards the German machine guns positioned in the sunken lane at Ficheux. Adams was awarded the MC for his command of D Company, the citation highlighting the attack on enemy machine gun posts and his personal reconnaissance, which he carried out on a bicycle. The citation concluded with, 'his total disregard of personal danger undoubtedly contributed largely to the steadiness of his company'.

When B Company and **Captain John Dempster** arrived at the level crossing they were ordered to hold the flanks on the Ficheux side of the railway. Here they were overrun by enemy tanks and it was during the ensuing fight that **Privates Herbert Watson and James Fullard** disabled an enemy tank at short range with a Boys rifle, their continuing fire at enemy armour contributed to the company being able to withdraw. What made their award of the Military Medal (MM) even more noteworthy was the fact that both men were wounded during the action and neither had previously fired the Boys rifle. From the white house walk down the disused road towards the railway line to where the level crossing once enabled the road to cross the railway line. There is little to see amongst the shrubs and trees bordering the line but some remnants of the old crossing are still visible.

After you have retraced your steps to your vehicle, continued downhill to the house on the right, which you will see just before the crossroads. There is room to pull off the road here. This is the former

The former home of the Cagin family marks the former turning to Ficheau and was where Second Lieutenant Stordy was ordered to secure the right flank at the junction of the road to Ficheux.

home of the Cagin family and where **Second Lieutenant Stordy** was ordered to secure the right flank at the junction of the road to Ficheux. The line of trees on the northern side of the house marks the route of the former road to Ficheux. In 1985 the crossroads was remodelled when the TGV railway bridge was added, dispensing with the level crossing and the staggered crossroads.

Now turn right along the D34 towards Ficheux. After some 600 yards you will see a track on the right just before a large factory complex, stop here. This is the approximate position where B and C Companies of the 10/DLI were attacked between the railway line and Ficheux after passing through B Company of the Tyneside Scottish. Not a single survivor remained from C Company and **Captain John Kipling** was killed. From this point you can see the high ground to the right where D Company, Tyneside Scottish, attacked. Continue into Ficheux, noting the openness of the ground on both sides of the road, for another 900 yards until you see a long redbrick building on your right. This is **Pronier Farm,** which is still much as it was in May 1940. Stop here. The houses on the opposite

The Pronier Farm is almost exactly as it was in May 1940.

side of the road were not built when Lieutenant Colonel Swinburne and his convoy reached this point, leaving the German machine gunners an uninterrupted field of fire from the sunken lane, which we will visit later. Swinburne, you will remember, was in advance of the remainder of the battalion, and was on his way to report to Brigadier Kircup at Barly when

The well head in the Pronier Farm that hid a British soldier during the encounter with the 8th Panzer Division.

the convoy came under fire at 9.15am near the Pronier Farm. His vehicle was bringing up the rear of the convoy when it was ambushed along the road between here and **Darras Farm**, [which is another 270 yards further along the road a few yards west of the left hand bend]. Pronier Farm is the approximate location described by **Private Malcolm Armstrong** as he evacuated his truck, leaving Private Arthur Todhunter dead inside the vehicle. After the engagement several men were buried inside the farm quadrangle.

From the Pronier Farm buildings continue to where the road bends round to the left, pausing to identify the **Darras Farm** before you bear left into Rue du 8 Mai 1945 and drive through the village to the next crossroads. Turn left onto **Rue de Boisleux** for 300 yards until you see a narrow metalled road on the left opposite a small bungalow. If you park here and walk along the road it quickly degenerates into a track and it was from this point that the German machine gunners had a clear field of fire across to the convoy as it passed Pronier Farm.

Return to your vehicle and leave the village, turning left at the next crossroads to find **Bucquoy Road Cemetery** on the left. There is ample parking here. The cemetery contains over 1,000 burials and commemorations of the First World War, of which 168 are unidentified. The cemetery was reopened again in May 1940 for the burial of troops killed during the German advance and the fighting around Ficheux. Of the 136 burials of the Second World War, twenty-six are unidentified and special memorials commemorate thirty-nine soldiers whose graves in the cemetery could not be specifically located. As you enter the cemetery the Second World War plot is on the right, contained in nine rows of headstones in front of the Cross of Sacrifice. Amongst the sixty-one identified men of the Tyneside Scottish are **Company Sergeant Majors John Morris** (6.I.13) and **Alfred Parmenter** (8.C.5), who were both killed after taking over Boys rifles whose crews had been killed. Both men were veterans of the previous war and John Morris had been awarded the Military Medal (MM). **Provost Sergeant Dick Chambers** (8.C.6) was killed near Pronier Farm as he attempted to fire his weapon through the observation visors of a German tank. **Lance Corporal Frederick**

The entrance to the sunken lane from where German machine gun teams were able to bring fire to bear on the Tyneside Scottish convoy as it passed the Pronier Farm.

Bucquoy Road Cemetery.

Laidler (8.E.6) played the regimental bagpipes that had been used in action at La Boisselle on 1 July 1916, until he too, was gunned down. Spare a moment for **Private Thomas Reed** (8.G.12), who was only 21-years-old when he was injured and run over by a tank. A former miner at Clara Vale Colliery, he was a member of the Ryton Holy Cross Church Choir before he joined up. It was not until 1946 that John and Isabella Reed learned of the circumstances of their son's death. 21-year-old **Private Albert Foster** (8.C.3), who was killed near Pronier Farm, died next to **Private Malcolm Armstrong** as they ran alongside the farm buildings. **Private Arthur Todhunter**, who was mentioned by Armstrong, is buried at Longuenesse Souvenir Cemetery, St Omer.

There are twenty-seven identified men of 10/DLI, who are all probably from B and C Companies and casualties of the attack that resulted in the demise of C Company and the death of its company commander, 37-year-old **Captain John Kipling** (8.E.9). The eight men from 11/DLI were possibly casualties of the

Private Thomas Reed

engagement at Wancourt. The only member of the Royal Tank Corps **is Second Lieutenant Walter 'Paddy' Nugent** (8.D.8), who was killed serving with 7/RTR on 21 May. Born in Yorkshire, the former Haileybury schoolboy was commissioned in 1938 and was the eldest son of Colonel W Nugent. The nine men from the AMPC were probably amongst those taken under Lieutenant Colonel Swinburne's command at Neuville-Vitasse, along with the four casualties from the RAOC. The pioneers tended to be much older men who were essentially non-combatants, although they were soldiers and therefore required to fight if necessary. The oldest is 50-year-old **Private William Wiltshire** (8.D.1) from South Ealing, a man who, I am sure, would have happily endorsed the second marriage of his wife Daisy to Albert Bloomfield in 1943. All of these men would have been in the convoy that was ambushed near Pronier Farm. In 1941 the men buried at the Pronier Farm were reinterred at the cemetery; there is no record available of who these men were.

Car Tour 2

Frankforce – The Left Flank Route

Start: Dainville Communal Cemetery
Finish: Tilloy-lès-Mofflaines
Distance: Eight miles

This car tour covers the left hand column's route taken by 4/RTR and 6/DLI on 21 May 1940. Sadly, much of the route from Dainville has been overtaken by the expansion of Arras which, together with the creation of new roads, has encroached across the line of advance used by the left column. This sprawling development persuades the battlefield tourist to use the D60 to avoid the prospect of navigating through Achicourt and Beaurains. We begin the tour at **Dainville Communal Cemetery** on the D59 **Avenue Lavoisier**, which is a short distance from the Faubourg d'Amiens in Arras. The cemetery contains thirty-eight burials from the First World War and 34-year-old **Sergeant Alfred Tinker** who was killed on 20 May 1940, serving with 92/Field Regiment. The main 1914-1918 CWGC plot is marked by the Cross of Sacrifice but the single 1940 burial is on the left, just a few yards inside the cemetery. It was at Dainville that elements of the 6th Rifle Regiment were engaged by 4/Northumberland Fusiliers

Dainville Communal Cemetery is on Avenue Lavoisier.

and 4/RTR. After leaving the cemetery continue west, towards the centre of Dainville, along Avenue Lavoisier to the roundabout where a left turn along Rue de Verdun will take you to a T Junction with the D265. Turn left and then first right to continue uphill along the D60, **Rue Georges Guynemer,** to a roundabout. At the roundabout take the *cul de sac* and pass beneath the metal barriers to visit the former level crossing where **Second Lieutenant Peter Vaux** and 4/RTR had a rather embarrassing incident while negotiating the steep embankments. Just on the other side of the level crossing 4/RTR ran into the flank of 6th Rifle Regiment.

The former level crossing where Second Lieutenant Peter Vaux and 4/RTR crossed the railway line at Dainville.

Return to the roundabout and follow the D60 for just under one mile until you reach the crossroads with the D3. Turn right, following signs for Agny Military Cemetery, and follow the road uphill to the next roundabout. Turn left here – signposted Agny – and follow the D60 over the next two roundabouts. At the third roundabout turn left onto the D917. You are now in the suburbs of Beaurains and across to your left, on **Rue Angele Richard,** are the CWGC buildings. 4/RTR was in this area and it was here that **Sergeant Major Jock Armit** fought his action against the German anti-tank guns. Continue until you reach a major crossroads with traffic lights. Turn right, [you will see numerous signposts but look out for Neuville-Vitasse and Croisilles] and stop, there is parking along here on the right. It was along this road, between Beaurains and Achicourt, that 6/DLI retired in the darkness of 21 May and where Y Company of the Northumberland Fusiliers, under the command of 29-year-old **Major Kenneth Clark**, came into action against units of the

The *Mairie* at Beaurains.

5th Panzer Division. **Lieutenant Thomas Bland** was killed along this road. The road today bears little resemblance to that of May 1940, which at the time was separated from Arras by an expanse of open country. Continue for another 500 yards to find the *Mairie* at Beaurains situated on your right, where there is parking on **Rue Victor Hugo** near to where the **Royal Tank Memorial** is situated. The memorial can be found in a small memorial garden to the right of the *Mairie*, and was inaugurated by Major General Dixon in May 1983. This rather grand memorial is constructed from cobbles and topped by a bronze model of a Matilda II. Surrounding the monument on three sides is a low wall on which tank tracks have been laid.

After leaving the garden drive back to the five-way intersection and take the road which is almost opposite the *Mairie* – **Rue du 1er Mai** – and continue to the mini roundabout, where the second exit will take you to the entrance gates outside **Beaurains Communal Cemetery,** where there is plenty of parking. The British graves are at the top end of the cemetery where you will find three casualties from the 4/RTR attack on 21 May, the most well known being 47-year-old **Major Gerald Hedderwick** who was commanding A Company of 7/RTR, but was on loan with his six Matilda IIs to bolster the strength of 4/RTR. Hedderwick had fought in the First World War, initially as an enlisted man, but was

The Royal Tank Memorial stands in a small garden on Rue Victor Hugo.

quickly commissioned into the Royal Scots, transferring to the Tank Corps in 1916. Awarded the MC in 1917, he played Rugby for the Army and was given a trial for the Scottish international side. In 1923 he returned to Loretto School in Musselborough to teach but, as a reserve officer, was called up in 1939. **Trooper George Mills** (A.3) and **Sergeant Sidney Temple** (A.1) are also recorded on the CWGC database as serving with 7/RTR, which makes it extremely likely that they were also from A Company, 7/RTR. The nine men from 6/DLI are recorded as being killed

Beaurains Communal Cemetery.

between 10 and 31 May 1940, which indicates they were buried in the cemetery well after the attack, as indeed were the two Northumberland Fusiliers. All of these men would have been part of the left hand column that attacked on 21 May. Buried in a single grave close by is **Pilot Officer James Caterer,** who was flying a Lancaster from 635 (Pathfinder) Squadron on the night of 16 June 1944 when the aircraft was shot down over Arras. Three other crew members were killed and are commemorated on the Runnymede Memorial, two evaded captivity, while the seventh was taken prisoner.

To return to the D60, continue along the **Route de Tilloy** for a further 200 yards to where you are required to turn right. Continue to the roundabout and return along the D60 towards Tilloy-lès-Mofflaines. Apart from the D60 being built right across the valley west of Telegraph Hill, the ground on both sides of the road is in a continual state of development and it is now difficult to stop to see the wooded crest of Telegraph Hill across to the right as you drive along the road. The best view of the hill and the shallow valley that runs down towards the D60 is from the exit to Tilloy-lès-Mofflaines; if you stop your vehicle on the waste ground just after you turn off you will have roughly the same view had by **Second Lieutenant Peter Vaux** of the knocked out tanks of 4/RTR that were strewn across the ground between here and Telegraph Hill. On the crest of the hill were 4th and 5th Batteries of *Generalmajor* Gottfried Frölich's AR 78; he had also positioned the 6th Battery on the road between Tilloy-lès-Mofflaines and Wancourt. It takes little imagination to understand why the 4/RTR attack was stopped here, particularly as the British 368/Battery was so ineffective. **Gerald Hedderwick** and **Lieutenant Colonel Fitzmaurice** were killed here, along with Fitzmaurice's operator, **Corporal Alan Moorhouse**.

Should you feel the need to get a closer view of Telegraph Hill you can walk along the track which takes you into the valley east of the hill and, incidentally, over the ground that once hosted the 1917 German defensive system called **The Harp**. Our route concludes in Tilloy-lès-Mofflaines, where, if you are lucky, refreshments can be found in the village centre.

Telegraph Hill is still crowned by a small copse.

Car Tour 3

Frankforce – The Right Flank Route

Start: Duisans British Cemetery
Finish: Wailly
Distance: Nine miles

This car tour covers the right hand column's route taken by 7/RTR and 8/DLI on 21 May 1940. The right hand route may have been less successful, but the path it followed from Duisans is far easier to follow by car. It is important to bear in mind that the 8/DLI did not even reach the start line and came under fire as far north as Maroeuil, where German gunners were ranging on the village. From Duisans, a minor road leads directly along the 8/DLI line of march to Warlus; we have deviated slightly to the west along the D62 in order to visit the communal cemeteries at Agnez-lès-Duisans and Warlus. As the battalion crossed the

The entrance to Duisans British Cemetery still shows the marks of battle received on 21 May 1940.

St-Pol road, the burnt out wreckage of a column of German 5.9-inch Howitzers was scattered around, along with dead and wounded German infantry, who had fallen prey to the armoured cars of Captains 'Dozy' Willis and Rupert Byass of C Squadron, 12/Lancers, and French tanks from 3/DLM.

We begin our tour at **Duisans British Cemetery**, which is situated on the D339 Arras to St-Pol road, there is parking by the entrance. Selected as a burial site by the 8th Casualty Clearing Station in 1917, the battlefield tourist will find no Second World War graves here and most of the 3,207 graves relate to the Battles of Arras in 1917. The damage to the stonework on the entrance gate was originally thought to have been the result of British anti-tank guns from 260/Battery engaging German armoured vehicles on 21 May 1940. However, as the cemetery gates face east, the 260/Battery guns are far more likely to have been positioned at the far end of the cemetery, which faces west. Not only does the entrance to the cemetery face east, but contemporary photographic evidence suggests that the cemetery was surrounded by a much higher hedge in May 1940, which would have considerably restricted any field of fire from the cemetery entrance. So what caused the damage to the stonework? Undoubtedly it was caused by French tanks firing on German infantry who were taking shelter in the cemetery. The German fugitives were most probably survivors from the destroyed artillery column that had run into British and French AFVs on the N39 Arras-St Pol road. It was from the steps leading into the cemetery that **Captain James Walton,** commanding C Company of the 8/DLI, noticed a German soldier peeping at him from behind a headstone. Shortly afterwards **Corporal George Self** and members of C Company were fired upon by enemy infantrymen, prompting them to clear the cemetery with the assistance of three French tanks.

With the entrance to the cemetery behind you, follow the road that leads back towards the D939/N39 and take the first road on the right – signposted D56 Agnez-lès-Duisans and Duisans. After a short distance you will come to the 18th century **Château du Duisans** on the right. There is limited parking by the River Gy. **Major Ross McLaren** based his headquarters at the château after **Lieutenant Colonel Beart** had left for Warlus with A and D Companies, the Carrier Platoon and part of HQ Company. McLaren's men took up defensive positions in Duisans while **Lieutenant John Leybourne** and some of B Company rooted out the German crews that remained at large around the château grounds after the incident on the St-Pol road. The château was also used as the Battalion Aid Post and was where **Lieutenant Wilkinson**, the battalion's medical officer, and the wounded remained after Major McLaren had withdrawn

Duisans Château.

the battalion to Maroeuil. Fortunately, McLaren writes in his diary, all the wounded were collected later. Another troop of 2-pounder anti-tank guns were positioned on the far side of the small wood behind the château; but it is not clear whether these were from the Brigade Anti-Tank Company or from 260/Battery.

Leave the château and continue to the crossroads. If you wish to inspect the church, which still bears the scars of 1940 battle damage and where German prisoners were kept in the small square opposite, then continue straight ahead, otherwise turn right and head towards **Agnez-lès-Duisans**.

It was at this point in 7/RTR's advance that they either took the wrong road or embarked on a short cut from Duisans to Wailly. But whatever the reason, they turned east through **Wagonlieu** towards Dainville, before turning south again towards Wailly, following a line of electricity pylons. At Dainville – much to their surprise – they bumped into the rear of 4/RTR, who had been clearing the village of Germans. As 7/RTR crossed the ridge at Wagonlieu, en-route to Dainville, they failed to see the 25th Panzer Regiment heading north from Beaumetz-lès-Loges to Acq. The

160

Germans apparently did not see the Matildas of 7/RTR and the two columns passed each other without a shot being fired!

Go through the village of Agnez-lès-Duisans, bearing left to take the Warlus road. As you leave the village the road rises and **Agnez-lès-Duisans Communal Cemetery** is on the right, marked by the French national flag. The three British graves are behind the French plot between the trees; one is unidentified. Both the identified men were killed serving with the 4/Northumberland Fusiliers and it is likely the unidentified man was from the same unit. 25-year-old **Fusilier Richard Pattison** and 27-year-old **Fusilier Robert Scott** are recorded on the CWGC database as being killed 20 May 1940, this is unlikely as the battalion was not in the area until the next day.

Agnez-lès-Duisans Communal Cemetery.

After leaving the cemetery continue along the road to Warlus. Half way along this road you will cross a gentle ridge and it was here that a troop of guns from 260/Battery engaged the **25th Panzer Regiment** as it returned from Acq. Slow down, as just before you enter the village **Warlus Communal Cemetery** is on the right. Go through the cemetery entrance and turn immediately left. The first headstone you come to is 35-year-old **Rifleman Albert Parker** of D Company, 7/King's Royal Rifle Corps, who was executed for desertion at dawn on 15 May 1916. Nearby is the second headstone, 21-year-old **Private Richard Cowe** of the 8/DLI, who was killed on 21 May 1940.

Leave the cemetery and, as you drive along the straight open road, Arras will be to your left. Continue directly through Warlus to the cross roads, passing the village war memorial on the left. The village was no stranger to the sight of British troops as it had hosted the headquarters of the British 14th (Light) Division in 1916 after they had taken over the trenches from 32nd French Division at Agny. One hopes that the British in 1916 were a little more organized than 7/RTR were in 1940, as by this time their tanks were becoming scattered across the open countryside. A few tanks from D Company headed towards Warlus while some, from B Company, moved parallel with the N25 to turn south east and advance towards Rommel's hill at le Belloy Farm. Others headed across the ridge towards Agny, with a few advancing towards Mercatel.

As you drive uphill from the war memorial you will soon reach the water tower on the left, which features in accounts of the battle; but beware, there is little room to park off the road here. This is the area in which Lieutenant Colonel Beart positioned the 8/DLI Headquarters [A and D Companies] and endured heavy dive bombing attacks from German aircraft before withdrawing back into the village. In one of the fields on the left was where Second Lieutenant Ian English pressed himself into the ground as the bombs fell all around him. On the water tower itself is a small plaque commemorating the men who fought and fell here in May 1940.

The water tower at Warlus on the D62 Route de Berneville. A plaque on the water tower commemorates the battle that was fought here (inset).

A set of steps takes the visitor into Berneville Communal Cemetery.

Continue through Berneville to the church, where a left turn along the D67 Rue d'Arras will take you to **Berneville Communal Cemetery**, which you will see on the left just beyond the bend in the road. Park immediately behind the calvary, near the football ground, and walk up the steps to the cemetery gates. There are three casualties from the First World War and four from the Second World War, which lie in the top right hand corner of the cemetery. Of these, **Drummer Frederick Rose**, 2/West Yorkshires, and **Private Ellis Holt**, 19/Manchesters, were both shot at dawn in March 1917. The two 8/DLI casualties were, in all probability, men from the A Company advance through Berneville on 21 May and 21-year-old **Private Adrian Wylie** may have died of wounds the following day while in captivity. 36-year-old **Flying Officer Gilbert Wright** was flying one of the four 605 Squadron Hurricanes that were lost on 22 May. Only two pilots managed to return to RAF Hawkinge via Dunkerque.

After leaving the cemetery return to the bend in the road and follow the D67 out of the village towards the N25, which you will see ahead of you on the rising ground. This was the view of the road that the men of

The D67 rises gently from Berneville to the junction with the N25, which was the start line for 8/DLI on 21 May.

A Company would have had on 21 May. Second Lieutenant Ian English tells us that they men were cheered up considerably when the road came into sight, 'knowing they were in sight of the start line'. Sadly, as we know, they were destined never to reach it. The N25 is where **Baron von Münchhausen** from the 7th Rifle Regiment was positioned when he was summoned by his battalion commander and ordered to clear Berneville with his company.

At the junction with the N25 turn right and then immediately left – signposted Wailly. Just before you reach Wailly Communal Cemetery, which you will see on your left, a narrow minor road doubles back on itself and leads to a collection of farm buildings. This is **le Belloy Farm**. Park your vehicle at the junction and walk up through the farm to the crossroads of tracks just beyond the farm buildings. It is always a good

Le Belloy Farm.

The track leading up to Hill 111 – known as Rommel's Hill.

idea to seek permission from the farmhouse. At the crosstracks turn right and walk uphill for approximately 300 yards; you will know when you have reached the summit of the hill when the ground falls away around you. This is spot height 111 on the IGN 1:50,000 map, where several German anti-tank and anti-aircraft guns were in position and where Rommel and his orderly officer, *OberLeutnant* Most, took up station near the quarry; demonstrating the value of forward command that was so characteristic of his style of leadership. Looking out over the battlefield, it is easy to imagine the Mark II Matildas of 7/RTR heading in this direction. Their thick armour was impervious to enemy anti-tank rounds

The view from Rommel's Hill looking northwest towards Warlus and Duisans.

Wailly Communal Cemetery. Is this the last resting place of Lieutenant Colonel Heyland?

and they were only stopped short of Hill 111 with the help of the nearby AR 78 artillery battery. *Oberleutnant* Most was killed here, falling mortally wounded next to Rommel; only a few days before, *Hauptmann* Schraepler, his ordnance officer, had been wounded in the arm when in a similar position. On both occasions Rommel escaped death by the skin of his teeth.

Retrace your steps and stop outside **Wailly Communal Cemetery**. As you enter the cemetery look half left to see the three British graves near the far wall. The two identified graves are those of 22-year-old **Trooper Alexander Arthur** of 7/RTR and 30-year-old **Sergeant Herbert Reppen**, also of 7/RTR, who were both killed on 21 May 1940. It is likely that these men were serving in B Company. There has been much controversy regarding the third unidentified grave of a British officer, which is said to be that of **Lieutenant Colonel Heyland**, the commanding officer of 7/RTR, who was killed near Wailly. The single French grave is that of **Lieutenant Roy Jacques**, a French tank officer killed on 21 May serving with 11/Royal Dragoons. Some sources suggest that *Oberleutnant* Most was temporarily buried here before being reinterred elsewhere.

Continue into Wailly, which was entered by Tom Craig in his Matilda II. His appearance caused havoc amongst the 7th Rifle Regiment, who were passing through the village. Had he but known it at the time, he was less than 1,000 yards from Rommel, who was conducting operations on Hill 111. Craig, after engaging the enemy, withdrew back to Achicourt. Our tour ends in Wailly from where, like Tom Craig, the D3 will take you back into Arras through Achicourt.

Other Cemeteries

A short distance from Warlus along the D59 is **Wanquetin Communal Cemetery Extension**. This is primarily a First World War cemetery that grew up around a casualty clearing station. However, there are nine Second World War burials, six of which are men of the 8/DLI who were killed on 21 May. Two are men from the 4/Northumberland Fusiliers who also were killed on the same day whilst serving with Z Company. **Private Robert McParlin** of the 11/DLI possibly died from injuries received while the battalion was providing working parties at Nuncq Airfield on 15 April 1940.

Wanquetin Communal Cemetery.

Appendix 1

German, British and French Tank Specifications

Panzer Kampfwaggon I		Panzer Kampfwaggon II	
Weight	5.4 tons	Weight	8.8 tons
Speed	25mph	Speed	25mph
Radius of Action	90 miles	Radius of Action	100 miles
Crew	2	Crew	3
Armament	2X7.9mm MG	Armament	1X20mm
			1X7.9mm MG
Armour	13mm/7mm	Armour	30mm/10mm

Panzer Kampfwaggon III		Panzer Kampfwaggon IV	
Weight	18 tons	Weight	20 tons
Speed	25mph	Speed	25mph
Radius of Action	100 miles	Radius of Action	125 miles
Crew	5	Crew	5
Armament	1X37mm	Armament	1X75mm
	3X7.9mm MG		2X7.9mm MG
Armour	30mm/10mm	Armour	30mm/8mm

Panzer Kampfwaggon 38(t)			
Weight	11 tons		
Speed	35mph		
Radius of Action	125 miles		
Crew	4		
Armament	1X37mm		
	2X7.9mm MG		
Armour	50mm/15mm		

Mark I Matilda		Mark II Matilda	
Weight	11 tons	Weight	26.25 tons
Speed	8mph	Speed	15mph
Radius of Action	80 miles	Radius of Action	60 miles
Crew	2	Crew	4
Armament	.303/.50-inch MG	Armament	2-pounder
Armour	60mm/10mm		1X.303-inch MG
		Armour	78mm/40mm

Light Tank Mark VIb	
Weight	5 tons
Speed	30/35 mph
Radius of Action	175 miles
Crew	3
Armament	1X50-inch MG
	1X.303-inch MG
Armour	14mm/4mm

Soma S35		Hotchkiss H35	
Weight	20 tons	Weight	10.5 tons
Speed	25 mph	Speed	16 mph
Radius of Action	144 Miles	Radius of Action	93 miles
Crew	3	Crew	2
Armament	1X47mm	Armament	1X37mm
	1XMG		1XMG
Armour	40mm	Armour	30mm

Appendix 2

Below is a list of cemeteries in the wider area of Arras that are outside the scope of this book but within a reasonable distance of central Arras. The 1939-1940 casualties buried in these, often quite isolated, cemeteries are very rarely visited by battlefield tourists. Some, like Fosseux, Cabaret Rouge British Cemetery and Hénin-sur-Cojeul Communal Cemeteries, contain only one or two graves, while others, such as Orchard Dump Cemetery, Avion and Écurie Communal Cemeteries, have larger concentrations. Further details can be found on the excellent CWGC website at: http://www.cwgc.org

Arleux-en-Gohelle Communal Cemetery
Avesnes-le-Comte Communal Cemetery Extension
Avion Communal Cemetery
Cabaret Rouge British Cemetery
Camblain-l'Abbé Communal Cemetery
Écurie Communal Cemetery
Fosseux Communal Cemetery
Givenchy-en-Gohelle Communal Cemetery
Habarcq Communal Cemetery Extension
Hénin-sur-Cojeul Communal Cemetery
Orchard Dump Cemetery, Arleux-en-Gohelle
Rouvroy South Communal Cemetery
Thélus Communal Cemetery

Appendix 3

Order of Battle– BEF at Arras 1940
GHQ Troops

Armoured	Infantry	Royal Artillery	Royal Engineers
12/Royal Lancers 4 and 7/Battalions Royal Tank Regiment	1/Welsh Guards **Pioneers:** 9/West Yorkshires	4/Anti-Aircraft Regiment, 1/Light Anti-Aircraft Regiment 5/Searchlight Brigade: 1,2,3/Searchlight Regiments	100/Army Field Coy 228, 242/Field Coys 223/Field Park Coy, 61/Chemical Warfare Coy

50th (Northumbrian) Division (With Frankforce 20-24 May)
Major General Giffard le Quesne Martel

150 Brigade	151 Brigade	25 Brigade	Motor Cycle infantry
GOC: *Brig C W Haydon* 4/ East Yorkshire 4/ Green Howards 5/ Green Howards	GOC: *Brig J A Churchill* 6/ Durham Light Infantry 8/ Durham Light Infantry 9/ Durham Light Infantry	GOC: *Brig W H C Ramsden* 2/ Essex Regiment 1/ Royal Irish Fusiliers 1/7th Queen's Royal Regiment	4/Royal Northumberland Fusiliers **Artillery** 72, 74/Field Regiments 65/Anti-Tank Regiment **Royal Engineers** 232, 505/Field Coys 235/Field Park Coy

23rd (Northumbrian) Division (with Petreforce 18-21 May subsequently with Rustyforce and III Corps)
GOC: Major General William Herbert

69 Brigade	70 Brigade	Motorcycle & MG Infantry	Royal Engineers
GOC: *Brig Viscount Downe* 5/East Yorkshire 6/Green Howards 7/Green Howards	GOC: *Brig P Kirkup* 10/DLI 11/DLI 1/Tyneside Scottish, (Black Watch)	8/Royal Northumberland Fusiliers 9/Royal Northumberland Fusiliers	233 and 507/Field Coys 508/Field Park Coy

5th Division (Released to GHQ Reserve and with I Corps 16-19 May, with Frankforce 20-24 May, with III Corps 24-25 May and then to II Corps from 25 May)
GOC: Major General Harold Franklyn

13 Brigade	17 Brigade	Artillery	Royal Engineers
GOC: *Brig M C Dempsy* 2/Cameronians 2/Royal Inniskilling Fusiliers 2/Wiltshire Regiment	GOC: *Brig M G N Stopford* 2/Royal Scots Fusiliers 2/Northamptonshire 6/Seaforth Highlanders	9, 91, 92/Field Regiments 52/Anti-Tank Regiment	38, 245 252/Field Coys 254/Field Park Coy

171

Select Bibliography

The National Archives
Unit War Diaries in WO 166 and 167.
Personal accounts in CAB 106 and WO 217.
POW Reports in WO 344, WO 373.

Imperial War Museum Sound Archive
Imperial War Museum Department of Documents
The National Army Museum
The RUSI Library

Published Sources
Anonymous, *Harder Than Hammers*, Tyneside Scottish Association 1947.
Baxter, I, *Blitzkrieg in the West*, Pen and Sword 2010.
Blaxland, G, *Destination Dunkirk: The Story of Gort's Army*, William Kimber 1973.
Dildy, D.C, *Fall Gelb 1940 (1)*, Osprey 2014.
Ellis, L.F, *The War in France and Flanders*, HMSO 1953
Ellis, L.F. *The Welsh Guards At War*, London Stamp Exchange 1989.
Farndale, M, *History of the Royal Regiment of Artillery*, Brasseys 1996.
Franklyn, Sir H, *The Story of One Green Howard in the Dunkirk Campaign*, Green Howards 1966.
Frieser, K-H, *The Blitzkrieg Legend*, Naval Institute Press 2012.
Hart, L, *The Rommel Papers*, Collins 1953.
Jackson, J, *The Fall of France*, OUP 2003.
Kemp, J.C, *The History of the Royal Scots Fusiliers 1919-1959*, Maclehose 1963.
Levine, J, *Forgotten Voices of Dunkirk*, Ebury 2010.
Lewis, P.J and English I.R, *8th Battalion The Durham Light Infantry 1939-1945*, N&M Reprint.
Lynch, T, *Dunkirk 1940 'Whereabouts Unknown'*, History Press 2010.
Macksey, K, *The Shadow of Vimy Ridge*, William Kimber 1965.
Murland, J. D, *Retreat and Rearguard: Dunkirk 1940*, Pen and Sword 2015.
Nightingale, P.R, *The East Yorkshire Regiment in the War 1939/45*, William Sessions 1952.
Perret, B, *Through Mud and Blood*, Robert Hale 1975.
Philson, A, *The British Army 1939-1945 Organization and Order of Battle Volume 6*, Military Press 2007.
Richard Holmes, *The Army Battlefield Guide, Belgium and Northern France*, HMSO 1995
Rissik, D, *The DLI AT War*, N&M Reprint.
Sebag-Montefiore, H, *Dunkirk – Fight to the Last Man*, Viking 2006.
Synge, W, *The Story of the Green Howards*, The Regiment 1954.
Thompson, J, *Dunkirk – Retreat To Victory*, Sidgwick and Jackson 2008.
Younger, T, *Blowing Our Bridges*, Pen and Sword 2004.
The Green Howards Regimental Newsletter, Issue 10, September 2000

Index

Craig, 2/Lt T., 57–8, 75–6, 167
Cullingford, Rev C., 38

Dainville, 50, 61, 69, 77, 152–3, 160
Darras Farm, 17, 148
Dempsy, Brig M., 90, 171
Donkin, Capt I., 84, 87–8
Doyle, Sgt B., 77, 79–80
Duisans, 52, 57, 66–8, 70–1, 74–5,
    158, 160, 165
Duisans, château at, 67, 75, 159–60
Dunkerque, 7, 8, 110–11, 113, 163
Dunn, 2/Lt J., 14, 16, 18, 142

English, 2/Lt I., 54, 57–8, 65, 67, 71–
    3, 75, 80, 162, 164
Eicke, *Obergruppenführer* T., 10

Fernie, Maj S., 50, 62
Ficheux, 14, 16–18, 20–2, 70, 75,
    141–2, 144, 146–7, 149
Fitzmaurice, Lt Col J., 50, 62, 108,
    157
Forrester, Maj H., 56
Franklyn, Maj Gen H., 5, 7–8, 10,
    41–2, 48–9, 82, 90, 98, 107
French Army Units and
Formations:
    3rd Light Mechanized Division, 9,
        66, 70, 74–5, 80, 159
    4th Regiment of Dragoons, 106
Furness, Lt C., 39–40, 43–5, 94, 135,
    139–40

Gamelin, Gen M., 1–2, 4, 7
German Army Units and
Formations:
Armoured Units:
    5th Panzer Division, 8, 10, 29, 63–
        4, 98, 111, 154
    7th Panzer Division, 9, 18, 22, 29,
        34, 49, 70, 74, 80, 109
    8th Panzer Division, 8–10, 12, 14,
        18–19, 65, 148
    25th Panzer Regiment, 9, 56, 68–
        70, 76, 109, 160–1
Motorized Units:
    6th Rifle Regiment, 9, 59, 152–3

7th Rifle Regiment, xiv, 9, 71, 76,
    164, 167
8th Motorcycle Battalion, 9, 16
11th Motorized Brigade, 29
20th Motorized Division, 10, 29, 111
SS-Totenkopf Division, 10, 22,
    70, 81, 143
Infantry Units:
    12th Infantry Division, 29, 111
    27th Infantry Regiment, 90–2
Artillery Units:
    42nd Anti-Tank Battalion, 77
    78th Artillery Regiment, xiv, 9
Giraud, Gen H., 2
Gort, 6th Viscount Vereker, 2–8, 12,
    36, 41, 43, 82, 107, 111
Griffin, Sgt G, 39, 43–4
Guderian, *Generalleutnant* H, 29, 49–
    50

Habarcq, 3–4, 81
Hartlieb-Walsporn, *Generalleutnant*
    M. von, 10
Hedderwick, Lt Col G., 51–2, 62,
    154, 157
Herbert, Maj Gen W., 11, 171
Heyland, Lt Col H., 53, 108, 166
Hinchcliffe, Lt Col J., 98–9, 101–103
Hôtel de l'Univers (Arras), 132–3
Houchin, Capt D., 99–103

Ironside, Gen Sir E., 3, 6–7, 12

Jardin de la Légion d'Honneur
    (Arras), 131

King, Maj J., 77–9
Kirkup, Brig P., 11–13, 16, 171
Kirby, Lt P., 84, 89
Kuntzen, *Generalleutnant* A., 9

Lacy, Maj W., 26,36
Lattre-St-Quentin, 14, 21–2, 28
Lefroy, Lt Col F., 84, 92
Leybourne, Lt J., 54, 56, 66–8
Llewellyn, Lt R., xvi, 31–2
Lloyd, Capt C., 23
Littleboy, Lt Col C., 84, 86, 88–9, 91

175

176